# Adult Museum Programs

*ABOUT THE SERIES*
The American Association for State and Local History Book Series publishes technical and professional information for those who practice and support history, and addresses issues critical to the field of state and local history. To submit a proposal or manuscript for the series, please request proposal guidelines from AASLH headquarters: AASLH Book Series, 1717 Church St., Nashville, Tennessee 37203. Telephone: (615) 320-3203. Fax: (615) 327-9013. Web site: www.aaslh.org.

*ABOUT THE ORGANIZATION*
The American Association for State and Local History (AASLH) is a nonprofit educational organization dedicated to advancing knowledge, understanding, and appreciation of local history in the United States and Canada. In addition to sponsorship of this book series, the Association publishes the periodical *History News*, a newsletter, technical leaflets and reports, and other materials; confers prizes and awards in recognition of outstanding achievement in the field; and supports a broad education program and other activities designed to help members work more effectively. To join the organization, contact: Membership Director, AASLH, 1717 Church St., Nashville, Tennessee 37203.

# Adult Museum Programs

## Designing Meaningful Experiences

Bonnie Sachatello-Sawyer
Robert A. Fellenz
Hanly Burton
Laura Gittings-Carlson
Janet Lewis-Mahony
Walter Woolbaugh

ALTAMIRA
PRESS

*A Division of Rowman & Littlefield Publishers, Inc.*
Walnut Creek • Lanham • New York • Oxford

ALTAMIRA PRESS
A division of Rowman & Littlefield Publishers, Inc.
1630 North Main Street, #367
Walnut Creek, CA 94596
www.altamirapress.com

Rowman & Littlefield Publishers, Inc.
A wholly owned subsidiary of The Rowman & Littlefield Publishing Group, Inc.
4501 Forbes Boulevard, Suite 200
Lanham, MD 20706

PO Box 317
Oxford
OX2 9RU, UK

British Library Cataloguing in Publication Information Available

**Library of Congress Cataloging-in-Publication Data**

Adult museum programs : designing meaningful experiences / Bonnie
Sachatello-Sawyer ... [et al.]
    p. cm. — (American Association for State and Local History book
series)
Includes bibliographical references and index.
ISBN 0-7591-0096-9 (alk. paper) — ISBN 0-7591-0097-7 (pbk. : alk.
paper)
1. Museums—Study and teaching—United States. 2. Museum
techniques—Study and teaching—United States. 3. Adult
education—United States—Curricula. 4. Non-formal education—United
States—Curricula. I. Sachatello-Sawyer, Bonnie, 1964- II. Series.
AM11 .A38 2002
069'.071'073—dc21
                                        2002001984

Printed in the United States of America

∞ ™ The paper used in this publication meets the minimum requirements of American
National Standard for Information Sciences—Permanence of Paper for Printed Library
Materials, ANSI/NISO Z39.48-1992.

Dedicated to Jean Thorson,
an extraordinary teacher who inspired this book

*When I do educational work with a group of people, I try to see with one eye where those people are as they perceive themselves to be. I do this by body language, by imagination, by talking to them, by visiting them, by learning what they enjoy and what troubles them. . . . You have to start where people are, because their growth is going to be from there.*

*Now my other eye is not such a problem, because I already have in mind a philosophy of where I'd like to see people moving. It's not a clear blueprint for the future but movement toward goals they don't conceive of at that time.*

—Myles Horton

# CONTENTS

# PREFACE

For more than a decade, I had the pleasure of working with adults who participated in the Museum of the Rockies' Paleo Field Program near Choteau, Montana. These people came to "dig dinos" for a week, arriving eager and excited, wearing new Indiana Jones–style field hats and hiking boots. The chance to dig was something they had dreamed of for a long time. Most had a passionate interest in geology or dinosaurs as children and were rekindling that interest as adults.

The Paleo Field Program was located in a spectacular and remote part of Montana. Against a backdrop of snow-capped mountains, the group settled into tipis, took their first steps into the badlands, and started to adjust to living and working outdoors. The first few days were often disorienting and physically challenging. A dry, hot landscape, blowing dust, temperamental sun showers, and personality differences posed challenges. By the third day, the atmosphere was noticeably different. Without television or other distractions, camp conversation grew rich and dynamic, as individual skills and past experiences became important. At times, everyone became a teacher and a student.

As rock and fossil discoveries were shared, so too were new perspectives. "Now I understand how rocks mark time," one participant reflected. "I also have more humility in recognizing how short a time any one person inhabits the planet. . . . This has been an awakening experience." Comments like this were the beginning of my realization that participants were learning about more than just fossils.

My interest in studying adult learning experiences began somewhere in the course of my work with the Paleo Field Program. In 1996, Dr. Robert Fellenz and I received a grant from the U.S. Department of Education's Field-Initiated Studies Program to explore the nature of museum programs for adults and identify what makes such programs not only successful, but transformative. With help from the American Association of Museums (AAM), the Association of Science-Technology Centers (ASTC) staff, and Museum of the Rockies director Arthur H. Wolf, we identified contacts at museums that offered a wide range of adult programs. Our research team expanded to include Hanly Burton and Laura Gittings-Carlson and graduate students Janet Lewis-Mahony and Walt Woolbaugh, each of whom was a valuable and equal contributor to the project.

Dr. Robert "Bob" Fellenz became the heart and soul of this research effort. He developed our protocols, conducted research, and trained the rest of the team to do the same. His experience as professor of adult education at Texas A. & M. and Montana State University and his special interest in adult learning enabled him to provide excellent guidance in all aspects of this project. Hanly Burton collected and analyzed the learning activities of program participants. Hanly's academic background in natural resource management and interpretation and his prior experience as education coordinator at Cave of the Mounds contributed to his many intelligent approaches to participant interviews and data analysis. Laura Gittings-Carlson had prior research experience in anthropology and had worked at the Museum for over five years in a variety of capacities, before joining the research team. Laura led the effort to interview program managers and did exceptional work as an interviewer and analyst. Janet Lewis-Mahony brought more than fifteen years of informal education and research experience with the National Park Service to the team. She worked diligently on all aspects of this project and completed a master's degree in adult and community education in the process. Walt Woolbaugh brought a wealth of formal teaching and research experience to the team as a junior high science teacher and an adjunct professor in science methods, assessment, and action research at Montana State University. He led the effort to interview contract instructors at museums and did an outstanding job. Everyone participated equally in the final research analysis and subsequent production of this book.

The project also greatly benefited from an advisory panel made up of adult-learning researchers, education department faculty, museum educators, and an independent evaluator. Advisers Becky Carroll, Gary Conti, Judy Diamond, Priscilla Lund, Sharon Horrigan, and Annie Storr reviewed the research plan, improved the research protocols, and kept us on track. Their advice and insight were crucial to our success.

Our study quantified a very exciting truth: museum programs can change people's lives. Effecting a positive change in an adult's life is a measurable goal that program planners can and do reach. It is our sincere belief that the challenge for museums in the twenty-first century is to create memorable experiences that inform, empower, and perhaps ultimately transform the lives of participants. We hope the insights offered by the program participants, instructors, and planners in this book will encourage professionals in all informal learning settings to reflect upon the value of museum experiences. Excellent adult learning programs benefit participants, museums, and society in the fullest sense.

Bonnie Sachatello-Sawyer

# ACKNOWLEDGMENTS

This study was made possible with a grant from the U.S. Department of Education's Field-Initiated Studies Program. We would like to especially thank program officer Delores Monroe for her excellent oversight and constant encouragement throughout this project.

Foremost, we would like to thank the hundreds of program participants, instructors, and museum professionals who allowed us to interview them. Also, special thanks to Bill Allen, Stephen Brand, Becky Carroll, Gail Cary, David Chittenden, Gary Conti, Judy Diamond, Lynn Dierking, Elizabeth Eder, John Falk, Karen Giles, Sharon Horrigan, Barbara Humes, Mary Hyman, Maury Irvine, Gretchen Jennings, Randi Korn, Ann Lockie, Priscilla Lund, Shelley McKamey, Francie McLean, Judy Meyer, Sally Middlebrooks, Mary Ellen Munley, Charles Sachatello, Dee Seitel, Bruce Selyem, Michael Spock, David Swingle, Annie Storr, Jean Thorson, Judy Weaver, Arthur H. Wolf, and Valerie Wheat for contributing their time and expertise.

We would like to thank Carol Inman, Susan Ewing, Samuel Taylor, Mitch Allen, Susan Walters, Pam Winding, the editors, and the anonymous reviewers at AltaMira Press for their critical reading of this manuscript and suggestions for improvement.

This project would not have been possible without the ongoing encouragement and expertise of the Museum of the Rockies' staff. We owe them a debt of gratitude for their continued support.

We would like to thank all of the museums in which we were allowed to conduct interviews and observe programs. They include: Albany Institute of History & Art, Amarillo Museum of Art, American Museum of Natural History, American Museum-Hayden Planetarium, Anchorage Museum of History and Art, the Andy Warhol Museum, Asian Art Museum of San Francisco, the Avery Brundage Collection, Austin Nature & Science Center, the Baltimore Museum of Art, Bayly Art Museum, Birch Aquarium at Scripps Institution of Oceanography, Birmingham Botanical Gardens, Bishop Museum, Bradbury Science Museum, Brookhaven National Laboratory Science Museum, Buffalo Bill Historical Center, Buffalo Museum of Science, Burke Museum of Natural History and Culture, Butterfly Pavilion & Insect Center, California Academy of Sciences, Canadian Museum of Civilization, Carnegie Museum of Art, Carnegie Museum of Natural History, Chicago Botanic Garden, Chula Vista Nature Center, the Cleveland Museum of Art, the Cleveland Museum of Natural History, Dallas Museum of Art, Decatur House Museum, Denver Art Museum, Desert Botanical Garden, Eiteljorg Museum of American Indians and Western Art, the Exploratorium, Fairfield Historical Society, Field Museum of Natural History, the Fine Arts Museums of San Francisco, M. H. De Young Memorial Museum, Florida Museum of Natural History, Florida Power and Light's Energy Encounter Museum, General Crook House Museum and Library/Archives Center, Georgia O'Keeffe Museum, Hagley Museum and Library, Hansen Planetarium, the Health Museum of Cleveland, the Henry Francis Du Pont Winterthur Museum, Inc., the High Desert Museum, Historical Museum at Fort Missoula, Historical Society of Western Pennsylvania, Houston Museum of Natural Science, Huntington Library, Art Collections, and Botanical Gardens, Huntsville Museum of Art, Idaho Museum of Natural History, Indiana State Museum, Institute for Learning Innovation, the J. Paul Getty Museum, the Jane Goodall Institute, Joslyn Art Museum, Kalamazoo Institute of Arts, Kansas University Natural History Museum and Biodiversity Research Center, Kimbell Art Museum, Lied Discovery Children's Museum, Los Angeles County Museum of Art, the Lyceum: Alexandria's History Museum, Mattress Factory, Ltd., the Metropolitan Museum of Art, Miami Museum of Science, Mingei International-Museum of Folk Art, the Minneapolis Institute of Arts, Missouri Botanical Garden, Modern Art Museum of Fort Worth, Montana Historical Society, Monterey Bay Aquarium, Morton Museum of Cooke County, Museum of Art and History at the McPherson Center, Museum of Church History and Art, Museum of Fine Arts, Museum of Fine Arts of St. Petersburg, Florida, Museum of Indian Arts & Culture/Laboratory of Anthropology, Museum of International Folk Art, Museum of New Mexico, Museum of Science, Museum of Science and Industry, Museum of Scientific Discovery, Museum of the City of New York, Museum of the Rockies, Mystic Aquarium and the Institute for Exploration, National Gallery of Art, National Museum of Wildlife Art, National Steinbeck Center, National Tropical Botanical Garden, Natural History Museum of Los Angeles County, Nevada State Museum and Historical Society, New Jersey Historical Society, Newseum, Northeastern Nevada Museum, Norton Simon Museum, Oakland Museum of California, Orlando Museum of Art, Pacific Science Center, Palm Springs Desert Museum, Inc., the Philadelphia Art Alliance, the Philbrook Museum of Art, Red Butte Garden, Reynolda House (Museum of American Art), Rochester Museum & Science Center, Rockwell Museum, Salt Lake Art Center, San Bernardino County Museum, San Diego Historical Society, San Diego Museum of Man, San Diego Natural History Museum, San Francisco Craft & Folk Art Museum, Sawtooth Science Center, the Science Museum of Minnesota, Scottsdale Museum of Contemporary Art, Sherman Library and Gardens, Skirball Cultural Center, South Florida Science Museum, the Speed Art Museum, St. Louis Science Center, Stuhr Museum of the Prairie Pioneer, Tucson Botanical Gardens, Tulsa Museum of Art, University of Colorado Museum, University of Oregon Museum of Art, University of Pennsylvania Museum of Archaeology and Anthropology, University of Wyoming Art Museum, Utah State Historical Society, Utah Museum of Fine Arts, Utah Museum of Natural History, Utah State Historical Society, Vancouver Art Gallery, Ventura County Museum of History & Art, Virginia Historical Society, Washington State Historical Society, Wheeler Historic Farm, Worcester Art Museum, Wyoming Territorial Prison and Old West Park, Yellowstone Art Museum.

A special thanks to the following individuals who supplied information for this book: Mark Morey, curator of education, Amarillo Museum of Art; Nathaniel Johnson, senior manager, Adult Education and Technical Services, American Museum of Natural History; Karen Cane, astronomy educator, American Museum—Hayden Planetarium; Sharon Abbot, curator of education, Anchorage Museum of History & Art; Jessica Arcand, curator of education, Andy Warhol Museum; Debra Clearwater, adult programs coordinator, Asian Art Museum of San Francisco, the Avery Brundage Collection; Janice Sturrock, education director, Austin Nature & Science Center; Bridget Globenski, programs director, Baltimore Museum of Art; Audrey Ann Wilson, director of education, Birmingham Botanical Gardens; Guy Kaulukukui, chairman of the Education Department, Bishop Museum; Janet Temple, director, Brookhaven National Laboratory Science Museum; Sharon Schroeder, director of education, Buffalo Bill Historical Center; Pat Schiavone, public programs manager, Buffalo Museum of Science; Judy Thaler, director of education, Buffalo Museum of Science; Diane Quinn, manager, educational programs, Burke Museum of Natural History & Culture; Annette Humphrey, adult/senior program coordinator, Butterfly Pavilion and Insect Center; Beth Mason, manager of adult programs, California Academy of Sciences; Marilyn Russell, curator of education and chair of Division of Education, Carnegie Museum of Art; Patty Jaconetta, program specialist for Adult Tours and Research, Carnegie Museum of Art; Charlene Shang Miller, education program specialist, adult programs, Carnegie Museum of Art; Cathy Andreychek, program specialist, Carnegie Museum of Natural History; Christine Mills, docent coordinator, Carnegie Museum of Natural History; Holly Estal, manager of continuing education, Chicago Botanic Garden; Barbara Moore, assistant director, Chula Vista Nature Center; Joellen DeOreo, associate director, Exhibitions & Adult Programs, Cleveland Museum of Art; Bob Segedi, education director, Cleveland Museum of Natural History; Scott Winterrowd, coordinator, Outreach Programs & Academic Courses, Dallas Museum of Art; Vas Prabhu, educational director, M. H. De Young Memorial Museum; Molly Keith Neal, director of collections and programs, Decatur House Museum; Joanne Mendes, coordinator of adult programs, Denver Art Museum; Pat Smith, assistant director of educational services,

Desert Botanical Garden; Paul Doherty, director of education, Exploratorium; Heather Alexander, curator of education, Fairfield Historical Society; Steve Bell, director of public programs, Field Museum of Natural History; Kristen Webber, manager of adult programs, Field Museum of Natural History; Betty Dunckel Camp, head of education, Florida Museum of Natural History; Pat Pixley, curator, General Crook House Museum and Library/Archives Center; Jackie M., education director, Georgia O'Keeffe Museum; Carol Hagglund, manager of interpretation and education, Hagley Museum and Library; Richard Cox, administrative manager, Hansen Planetarium; Bettie Carter, manager for adult programs, Health Museum of Cleveland; Rosemary T. Krill, curator of education, Henry Francis Du Pont Winterthur Museum, Inc.; Beth Twiss-Garrity, curator of education (teacher programs), Henry Francis Du Pont Winterthur Museum, Inc.; Holly Remer, director of education, the High Desert Museum; Darla Bruner, education curator, Historical Museum at Fort Missoula; Ann Fortescue, director of education, Historical Society of Western Pennsylvania; David Temple, education director, Houston Museum of Natural Science; Sue Lafferty, director of education, Huntington Library, Art Collections, and Botanical Gardens; Mickey Heydorff, volunteer coordinator, Huntington Library, Art Collections, and Botanical Gardens; Deborah Taylor, director of education, Huntsville Museum of Art; Stefan Sommer, curator of entomology, ecology, and community outreach, Idaho Museum of Natural History; Cynthia Ewick, curator of education, manager of education services, Indiana State Museum; Karen Giles, manager, Adult and Community Audiences, the J. Paul Getty Museum; Nancy Rounds, acting curator of education, Joslyn Art Museum; Dena Podrebarac, assistant director for public affairs, Kansas University Natural History Museum and Biodiversity Research Center; Brad Kemp, public education programs specialist, Kansas University Natural History Museum and Biodiversity Research Center; Mary Barlow, education coordinator, Kimbell Art Museum; A. J. Rhodes, director of education, Lied Discovery Children's Museum; Anne Mumm, marketing and visitor services assistant/volunteer coordinator, Lied Discovery Children's Museum; Mary Martz, coordinator, Arts for All Program, Los Angeles County Museum of Art; Ximena Minotta, senior education coordinator, Los Angeles County Museum of Art; Margaret Pezulla-Graham, assistant museum educator (Evenings for Educators), Los Angeles County Museum of Art; Jenny Siegenthaler, associate museum educator (Teachers Academy), Los Angeles County Museum of Art; James C. Mackay III, director, the Lyceum: Alexandria's History Museum; Elvira Finnigan, education coordinator, Mattress Factory, Ltd.; Kent Lydecker, director of education, Metropolitan Museum of Art; Mathew James, public programs assistant for adult programs, Minneapolis Institute of Arts; Glenn Kobb, institutional coordinator for adult education, Missouri Botanical Garden; Terry Thornton, curator of education, Modern Art Museum of Fort Worth; Kristin Gallas, education officer, Montana Historical Society; Rita Bell, educator programs manager (Teacher Institute), Monterey Bay

Aquarium; Shana Powell, curator, Morton Museum of Cooke County; Celeste De-
Wald, programs education curator, Museum of Art & History at the McPherson
Center; Jenny Lund, curator of education, Museum of Church History and Art;
Lorri Berenberg, associate director for outreach, Division of Education and Public
Programs, Museum of Fine Arts; Rebecca Russell, curator of education, Museum of
Fine Arts of St. Petersburg, Florida; Fran Parson, docent organizer, Museum of Fine
Arts of St. Petersburg, Florida; Carol Cooper, curator of education and programs,
Museum of Indian Arts & Culture/Laboratory of Anthropology; Laura Temple-
Sullivan, director of education, Museum of International Folk Art; Sue Sturtevant,
chief of education, Museum of New Mexico; Brent Jackson, director of travel programs, Museum of Science—Boston; Paul Fontaine, director of public and school
programs, Museum of Science—Boston; Kathy Benson, education director, Museum
of the City of New York; Dee Seitel, volunteer coordinator, Museum of the Rockies; Kathy Lepore, director of education, Mystic Aquarium and the Institute for Exploration; Lynn Russell, head, adult programs, National Gallery of Art; Ann Hen-
derson, head of teacher programs, National Gallery of Art; Julie A. Springer,
coordinator of teacher programs, National Gallery of Art; Elaine Walsh-Partridge,
adult education manager, National Museum of Wildlife Art; Celeste DeWald, curator of education and public programs, National Steinbeck Center (formerly of the
Museum of Art & History at the McPherson Center); Anne O'Malley, senior in-
terpreter/programs coordinator, National Tropical Botanical Garden; Isabel Rosen-
baum, volunteer programs coordinator, Natural History Museum of Los Angeles
County; Barbara Slivac, curator of education, Nevada State Museum & Historical
Society; Jan Petersen, program coordinator, Northeastern Nevada Museum; Nancy
Gubin, director of educational programs, Norton Simon Museum; Barbara Henry,
chief curator of education, Oakland Museum of California; Sidney Williams, director of education and programs, Palm Springs Desert Museum, Inc.; Emily Good-
win, program coordinator, Philadelphia Art Alliance; Dick Hildreth, director of education, Red Butte Garden and Arboretum; Adrienne Cachelin, manager of natural
science education, Red Butte Garden and Arboretum; Nick Braggs, executive director, Reynolda House (Museum of American Art); Marjorie Northrup, assistant director for programs, Reynolda House (Museum of American Art); Kathleen Hut-
ton, coordinator of education, Reynolda House (Museum of American Art);
Ramona Englebreck, coordinator of adult programs, Rochester Museum & Science
Center; Jenny Monroe, supervisor, public programs, Rockwell Museum; Rebecca
Campbell, curator of education, Salt Lake Art Center; Jolene Redvale, education director, San Bernardino County Museum; Linda Canada, education coordinator, San
Diego Historical Society; Angelica Docog, director of education, San Diego Museum of Man; Dee Norton, program coordinator, education, San Diego Natural History Museum; Pat Flanagan, director of education, San Diego Natural History Museum; Margaret Kadoyama, education coordinator, San Francisco Craft & Folk Art

Museum; Chris Gertschen, director and founder, Sawtooth Science Center; David Chittenden, vice president of education, Science Museum of Minnesota; Bill Allen, manager of adult programs and tours, Science Museum of Minnesota; Tessa Bridal, director of public programs, Science Museum of Minnesota; Jane Wangberg, director of volunteers, Science Museum of Minnesota; Ruth Ladwig, exhibit gallery supervisor, Science Museum of Minnesota; Caroline Robbins, director of education, Scottsdale Museum of Contemporary Art; Wade Roberts, garden director, Sherman Library & Gardens; Adele Lander-Burke, director of museum instruction and education, Skirball Cultural Center; Michele Turner, director of education, South Florida Science Museum; Dale Clark, director of education, Stuhr Museum of the Prairie Pioneer; Meg Quinn, education director, Tucson Botanical Gardens; Holly Coons, curator of education, Tulsa Museum of Art; Lauren Schwartz, director of public programs, University of Colorado Museum; Lisa Abia-Smith, director of educational outreach, University of Oregon Museum of Art; Caci Manning, public relations coordinator, University of Oregon Museum of Art; Deborah Carl, outreach coordinator, University of Oregon Museum of Art; Gillian Wakely, assistant director for education, University of Pennsylvania Museum of Archaeology and Anthropology; Scott Boberg, curator of education, University of Wyoming Art Museum; Bernadette Brown, curator of education, Utah Museum of Fine Arts; Claudia Oakes, assistant director for operations (Museum & Hansen Planetarium), Utah Museum of Natural History; Beth Steele, administrative manager of museum education, Utah Museum of Natural History; Cheryl Sneddon, museum education curator, Utah State Historical Society; Alexis O'Neil, education director, Ventura County Museum of History & Art; Bill Obrochta, education director, Virginia Historical Society; Pat Blankenship, director of museum services, Washington State Historical Society; Glenn Humphreys, curator director, Wheeler Historic Farm; Claire Loughheed, assistant director of education, Worchester Art Museum; Pam Malone, executive director, Wyoming Territorial Prison and Old West Park; Becky Davis, curator of education, Yellowstone Art Museum; Len Adams, Community Leadership Supervisor, Pacific Science Center.

# INTRODUCTION

A coherent, diverse list of offerings helps us make more of the museum's resources available to the public. Exhibits alone can't touch the wealth of information and expertise housed here.

—Diane Quinn, manager of educational programs,
Burke Museum of Natural History and Culture

Museum programs attract hundreds of thousands of mature learners each year. They come to learn something new, to be entertained, and to socialize. Many are seeking experiences that can lead to personal growth and transformation. Museums have a tremendous potential to serve the education and personal growth needs of these adult learners. When administered well, adult museum programs can pay for themselves, build family and community involvement, encourage museum patronage, and promote lifelong learning, while providing role models for young people.

*Adult Museum Programs: Designing Meaningful Experiences* is based on the premise that excellent museum programs can change people's lives. Confirmation of this came from a three-year research study, conducted among adults in many types of museums across the United States, in which the attributes of excellence were framed. In these pages, you will find chapters that describe certain excellent programs, articulate the characteristics and categories of adult learners and instructors in museums, and make recommendations for creating programs to match mature learners' needs. Insights about excellence and adult programs are offered by adult-learning experts, museum education specialists, course instructors, and program participants. We want to share their "voices of experience" with readers interested in promoting adult learning through museum programs.

Funding for this study came from the U.S. Department of Education, Division of Post-Secondary Education, Field-Initiated Studies Research Program. This innovative move by the division demonstrated recognition of the impact that informal education has on our country's adult population. Museums, libraries, and the emerging resources of the Internet together with the more traditional resources of newspapers, magazines, and television provide an important informal learning network for adults.

## Prior Research on Adult Museum Programs

In the past three decades, significant professional studies have examined adults' motivations for participating in museum programs. Marilyn Hood identified six criteria that individuals used when judging leisure activities,[1] including:

- Being with people, or social interaction
- Doing something worthwhile
- Feeling comfortable and at ease in one's surroundings
- Having a challenge of new experiences
- Having an opportunity to learn
- Participating actively

Similar criteria have been identified by others investigating successful adult learning experiences.

Over the past two decades, research in museum education has increasingly focused on the needs of the learners. From this we have gained new insights on the learning styles and needs of children, family groups, and adult learners.[2] However, museum professionals continue to struggle with descriptions, measurements, dimensions, and values of learning in museums. Most agree that museums have the capacity to affect an individual's knowledge, skills, attitudes, beliefs, feelings, and concepts. Museums can even provoke life-changing experiences.[3] The nature of museum learning is indeed broad, rich, and multifaceted.

Research findings reveal that museum learning includes behavioral traits (skill building and physical training); cognitive attributes (comprehending information and organizing it); affective attributes (encompassing self-confidence, attitudes, emotions, spirituality, and personal growth); and social attributes (interaction, interpersonal relationships, civic pride, and cultural and community values). Learning involves the negotiation of meaning as adults make sense of scholarly interpretation through the lens of their own experience.[4] It involves valuing nature, humankind, exquisite objects, history, ideas, the unique, and the mundane. As Mihaly Csikszentmihalyi and Kim Hermanson maintain,

> Learning involves an open process of interaction with the environment. This experiential process develops and expands the self, allowing one to discover aspects of one-

self that were previously unknown. Thus, the learning experience involves the whole person, not only the intellectual, but the sensory and emotional faculties as well.[5]

Several studies on family learning in museums have analyzed the role of parents in informal education settings. For example, Judy Diamond has described the powerful impact of shared museum experiences and the contributions of individual family members.[6] John Falk and Lynn Dierking have described parent and child museum recollections.[7] In studying adult and child interactions, Minda Borun and her colleagues developed a useful protocol to describe different levels of family learning in exhibits.[8]

Until recently, little research has focused on adult museum programs. In 1975, Mary Hyman of the Maryland Academy of Sciences studied the status of adult programs in science centers. In a survey of science museum professionals, she found that 80 percent of educational programming was aimed at children, while just 20 percent was directed toward adults—a clear indication that science centers have "justifiably been considered 'children's museums' by the general public."[9] At most, science centers were considered "family-oriented."[10]

In 1995, Bonnie Sachatello-Sawyer initiated another survey to assess the types of adult museum programs taking place, to delineate the predominant teaching styles used by museum educators with adults, and to determine how adult education methodology is used in program design and planning.[11] This research project surveyed 110 museum educators from a wide variety of museums that were members of either the American Association of Museums or the Association of Science-Technology Centers. Data from this study illuminated the status of adult museum programs in the United States and how well they utilized adult education methodology in learning situations.

Of the 110 museum educators who completed the 1995 survey, 94 percent noted that they offered some type of adult museum program. But when asked what percentages of their total museum education programs were designed for adults, families, and children, they reported on average that only 27 percent of their programs were designed for adults, while 24 percent were designed for families and 49 percent were designed for children. "Child-oriented museums" made up 77 percent of all museums surveyed. "Adult-oriented museums" made up only 16 percent of the population. These museums created fewer children's programs and offered more programs for adults, including lectures, tours, gallery demonstrations, volunteer-training courses, and discussion groups. Different types of museums (e.g., art museums, history museums, science centers) were found in both groups.

## Real Stories, Real People: Our Research Design

For our national study of adult museum programs, we chose a qualitative approach to the research and followed the general principles of naturalistic inquiry advocated by Edward Guba,[12] Robert Bogdan and Sara Biklen,[13] and Sharon Merriam.[14] Naturalistic inquiry uncovers important, idiosyncratic stories told by real people about real events, in real and natural ways.[15] From the very beginning of this project, we wanted the "important stories told by real people" to be heard. A complete set of all of the interview protocols that we developed can be found on our Web site: www. realexperiencesinc.com.

As adult educators working with adult learners, we were also guided by Merriam's six principles of qualitative case-study design. Such research (1) is concerned more with process than product; (2) is grounded in the search for meaning, or how people make sense of themselves and the world; (3) makes the researcher, rather than an inventory or questionnaire, the primary instrument in collecting and analyzing data; (4) involves field work in a natural setting; (5) is descriptive; and (6) builds concepts from details inductively. These principles also fit well with the guidelines for naturalistic research published by the U.S. Department of Education.

Between 1996 and 1999, our research team scattered across the country to examine a variety of successful adult museum programs. We were particularly interested in identifying and measuring the personal, transformative effect programs had on adults. In all, we interviewed 508 museum program participants, 75 instructors, and 143 museum program planners in all types and sizes of museums, including art institutes, natural and cultural history museums, science centers, historical homes, and botanic gardens. Our team studied a wide array of programs in various formats, including credit and noncredit classes, lectures, symposia, field trips, guided tours, gallery demonstrations, discussion groups, volunteer-training courses, teacher workshops, film series, and dramatic presentations. Adults were defined broadly to include mature individuals who freely chose to participate in leisure learning activities.

Three primary questions drove our study:

1. From participants' perspectives, what constitutes an excellent museum program for adults?

2. What teaching strategies are employed in successful and innovative museum programs?

3. Does the informal learning environment of a museum add anything unique to the adult learning experience?

Preparation for addressing these questions included an extensive review of the literature in the fields of adult and museum education. Then interview schedules were created, tested, and revised. Systems for data storage and manipulation were selected. Only then could the exciting task of visiting museums, observing programs, and interviewing museum educators begin. In addition, our research team informally discussed many issues with museum educators at varied conferences and during visits.

## Implementing the Project

In the first year, we focused on twelve museums: the Buffalo Museum of Science, the California Academy of Sciences, the Chicago Botanic Garden, the Field Museum of Natural History, the Museum of the Rockies, Boston's Museum of Science, the University of Oregon Museum of Art, the Reynolda House Museum of American Art, the San Diego Natural History Museum, the Museum of Art and History at the McPherson Center, the Science Museum of Minnesota, and the Washington State Historical Society.

These museums were chosen from an initial list of 114 institutions identified by peers as having excellent adult programs. In whittling the list to a representative dozen, we looked at the size and type of the museum, diversity of program offerings, geographic location, and the museum's willingness to participate in the three-year study. Additional museums participated in the second and third years of the study, as time and resources allowed. All of the museums participating in this study were members of either the American Association of Museums or the Association of Science-Technology Centers.

One or more members of the research team visited each of the twelve museums at least once. Researchers interviewed program managers and observed programs firsthand. When opportune, teachers and participants were interviewed on-site. We attempted to interview three participants from the same class; when three on-site interviews could not be accomplished, museum staff provided the names of program participants willing to be interviewed by phone. Most phone interviews lasted ten to fifteen minutes, while face-to-face interviews sometimes lasted an hour or longer.

In addition to interviews conducted with program managers from the twelve selected museums, we also contacted other program managers through the *Official Museum Directory*. To assure a diverse sample, we approached individuals from nearly every state, representing museums of all types and sizes. These phone interviews averaged fifty minutes in length.

In the end, our research team interviewed 143 museum program planners from 116 different museums, including curators of education, directors of education, adult education program planners, and curators of education and public programming. When a museum had no education or public programming department, we interviewed the individuals in charge of adult programs. Through these interviews, we attempted to answer five major questions:

- Why are adult programs offered in museums?

- What different types of programs are offered?

- How are instructors selected, where are they found, and what guidelines are they given?

- What are the barriers to offering excellent adult programs?

- What constitutes an excellent adult museum program?

Researchers also managed to interview seventy-five contract and museum-based adult education instructors, though arranging interviews with instructors often proved difficult. Often, instructors were engaged with participants after class, and it was hard to reach instructors by phone because of their work commitments. When we did catch up with them, interview sessions varied from ten minutes to an hour in length.

Researchers entered their notes into a FileMaker Pro computer file. Microsoft Excel and Statistical Package for Social Sciences (SPSS) softwares were also used for data collection and analysis. (Only a small number of interviews were audio or video recorded.) Research team members and members of our advisory committee repeatedly reviewed and discussed data and interim conclusions were presented to outside audiences for additional input.

## In a Nutshell: What We Learned

Our study found that 94 percent of museums offer some type of adult programming, and these museums are offering more adult museum programs than ever before. Even as the numbers of programs are increasing, however, many museums are struggling to market or deliver programs that adults are interested in and willing to pay for. A few museums are even eliminating adult programs because they have failed to attract new audiences or are deemed financially nonviable.

Within the realm of adult museum programs, there are varied and conflicting needs and value systems. From an institutional perspective, the value of adult programs is typically based on the program's ability to earn money and serve large numbers of people. Not surprisingly, lectures are the most common adult program offering. But from an adult program participant's perspective, dull lectures are out, unique and active learning experiences are in.

Most program participants want more access to unique people, places, and objects. An excellent museum program, however, is first and foremost a learning opportunity. Adults demand to *learn* something from museum programs. They may object to hard chairs and lectures delivered in a monotone, but such factors are forgiven when good teaching and learning exchanges take place.

Many adults initially sign up for programs with only general goals in mind, such as learning to identify birds or tracing the settlement of their community. Yet such programs are rated most highly when they lead not only to new skills but to new perspectives, attitudes, insights, and appreciations. Our research team believes personal transformation is an important, and previously overlooked, measure of program excellence and we encourage museums and program planners to make every effort to recognize and achieve that goal.

## The High Points

- Adult programs are now common in all types of museums

- Adults today are more educated than ever, enlarging the pool of likely museum program-goers

- Museums are well positioned to deliver the mediated experiences baby boomers crave

- Adult programs can pay for themselves and encourage repeat visitation

- A key to understanding adult program choices can be found in an examination of their childhood interests

- Collaborative adult programs strengthen our communities

- Excellent adult programs change peoples' lives

## Typical Difficulties

- High staff turnover among museum educators adversely affects an institution's ability to develop ongoing relationships with its core audience of adults

- Educators often view themselves as second-class citizens or as powerless to improve adult experiences within an institution

- Education and marketing departments often do not coordinate their work

- Administrations set expectations for adult programs without providing adequate resources

- Internal evaluations tend toward retaining adult programs that are "cash cows" rather than those that deliver long-term learning outcomes

- Adult programs are not attracting culturally or socioeconomically diverse audiences

- Contract instructors often do not connect the course material to the museum's mission and vision

- To develop programs, most program planners still rely on personal experiences instead of audience-driven evaluation results and marketing studies

*continued*

*continued*

- Staff rarely take full advantage of the museum's resources when developing adult programs

- Museum programs are all too often viewed as a "nuisance" by staff outside of the education department

- While some larger museums have hired adult educators to develop adult programs, most museum educators have little or no training in adult education

### What Constitutes an Excellent Program?

Excellent museum programs change adult lives. These programs transform adults by motivating them to pursue new learning activities and continue to influence adults' future decisions about learning long after the program's end.

As learning experts Lisa Roberts[16] and Jack Mezirow[17] argue, the ultimate goal of learning is to create meaning in our lives or integrate a new insight into an existing base of knowledge. For example, as one participant noted in a landscape design class, "I'll remember the first part of the class, when the instructor took us around the botanic garden and opened my eyes to seeing the garden in a whole new way. I was able to compare and contrast the landscaping in the botanic garden with my yard at home. I can use landscaping ideas from the botanic garden in the landscaping around my own home."

### What Teaching Methodologies Are Used in Successful Programs?

Museum adult education programs are taught by a variety of instructors who use many teaching methods. No one methodology works better than others for all situations. Instructors who relate to the needs and interests of learners and present content knowledge in an enthusiastic manner in participatory settings seem to enjoy the most success. These instructors come from diverse backgrounds and teach for a number of reasons.

Outstanding instructors may be schoolteachers, college professors, local hobbyists, or members of a museum staff. They generally teach their particular class in more venues than just museum settings. Their reasons for teaching are varied, but they all have a passion for their subject, combined with a strong desire to share this information with other people.

Instructors who are able to integrate museum materials with good teaching strategies can help learners discuss, reflect upon, and apply new insights to all areas of their lives. Museum programs become dynamic learning situations when participants leave classes with lifetime learning goals. Instructors who take the time to identify good androgogical techniques, who remain current in their knowledge area, and who act as self-reflective practitioners will lead sessions that are productive for both themselves and their participants.

Many of the adult participants supported the idea that it is the relationship of the teacher to the learner, rather than simply the words presented, that lead to learning. Teaching is an art that is appreciated by adult learners. Good teaching techniques not only promote attendees' learning but also affect their expectations when they attend other educational activities.

As a museum tour participant observed, "The tour leader promoted such interaction and sharing among the group members that she thought we were all part of a family by the end of the tour. She led in a way that promoted a feeling of openness."

### Does a Museum Offer Anything Unique for Adult Learners?

"I'll remember that the instructor did a great job," one adult learner commented. "Instead of using pictures of birds, he used the actual preserved specimens." Museums offer access to unique objects, unique people, and unique places, and it is through this access that museums can offer unusual and valuable learning opportunities. Collections are especially powerful tools for providing adults with new personal experiences. For example, at the saki tasting class at the Seattle Asian Art Museum, instructors created an indelible experience for participants by using porcelain pieces from their collections to serve the saki.

The overall environment of a program can also catalyze change and have a lasting effect on participants. Sights, smells, and sounds all combine to create a memorable atmosphere for many museum programs. Program participants at a maple-sugaring event held in a state park remarked often of the beauty of the area and of the snow falling as they walked around, learning about the process of making maple syrup and maple sugar. At a program on medicinal uses of native plants, program participants were encouraged to "look at this flower, touch its leaves, smell its fragrance, and finally, taste its petals." The powerful taste of wild garlic flowers and the overall multisensory approach were indeed memorable and contributed significantly to the success of the program.

## Read On!

We hope that this book will help you find ways to create programs that satisfy, challenge, and even transform the adult learners in your community. We invite you to "pick and choose" your way through the book and we hope you return to it often for information and inspiration. The structure of the book is as follows:

- Chapter 1 introduces adult learners. We see how they learn and examine their motivations as we present several major *conclusions* derived from our study.

- Chapter 2 discusses the *basic methodology* of adult museum programs and shares idea-provoking examples of excellent programs.

- Chapter 3 examines museum programs from the *participant's perspective*.

- Chapter 4 looks at programs from the *instructor's perspective*.

- Chapter 5 explores programs from the *program planner's perspective*.

- Chapter 6 focuses on recommendations for *designing meaningful experiences*.

As you read, we encourage you to dream a little, take some risks, and set expectations for adult programs a notch higher.

## Notes

1. Marilyn Hood, "Adult Attitudes toward Leisure Choices in Relation to Museum Participation" (Ph.D. diss., Ohio State University, 1981).

2. John Falk and Lynn Dierking, "Recalling the Museum Experience," in *Transforming Practice: Selections from the* Journal of Museum Education *1992–1999*, ed. J. S. Hirsch and L. H. Silverman, 268–277 (Washington, D.C.: Museum Education Roundtable, 2000).

3. Michael Spock and Debra Perry, "Listening to Ourselves: The Stories Museum People Tell and Their Implications for What Really Matters in Our Work" (paper presented at the annual meeting of the American Association of Museums, Atlanta, Ga., 1997).

4. Lisa Roberts, *From Knowledge to Narrative: Educators and the Changing Museum* (Washington, D.C.: Smithsonian Institution Press, 1997).

5. Mihaly Csikszentmihalyi and Kim Hermanson, "Intrinsic Motivation in Museums: What Makes Visitors Want to Learn?" *Museum News* 74, no. 3 (1995): 35.

6. Judy Diamond, "The Behavior of Family Groups in Science Museums," *Curator* 29, no. 2 (1986): 139–54.

7. Falk and Dierking, "Recalling the Museum Experience," 268.

8. Minda Borun, M. Cleghorn, and A. Chambers, "Families Are Learning in Science Museums," *Curator* 39, no. 2 (1996): 123–38.

9. Mary Hyman, *Adult Education Survey* (Washington, D.C.: Association of Science-Technology Centers, 1976), 8.

10. Hyman, *Adult Education Survey*, 9.

11. Bonnie Sachatello-Sawyer, "Coming of Age: The Status of Adult Education Methodology in Museums" (Ph.D. diss., Montana State University, 1996).

12. Edward Guba, *Toward a Methodology of Naturalistic Inquiry in Education Evaluation* (Los Angeles: University of California, Center for the Study of Evaluation, 1978).

13. Robert C. Bogdan and Sara K. Biklen, *Qualitative Research for Education: An Introduction to Theory and Methods* (Boston: Allyn and Bacon, 1992).

14. Sharon Merriam, *Case Study Research in Education: A Qualitative Approach* (San Francisco: Jossey-Bass, 1988).

15. Guba, *Naturalistic Inquiry*, 3.

16. Roberts, *From Knowledge to Narrative.*

17. Jack Mezirow, "Contemporary Paradigms of Learning," *Adult Education Quarterly* 46, no. 3 (spring 1996): 158–73.

# CHAPTER ONE

# ADULT LEARNERS: UNIQUE AUDIENCE, UNIQUE OPPORTUNITY

Adult learning experiences will become one of the largest growing areas of informal learning in the next twenty years.

—Stephen Brand, The New Enterprise Factory, Inc.

## Why Adult Learning?

The recently and soon-to-be retired population is and will be the healthiest, wealthiest, most-educated, and active population of nonworking adults we have ever seen in America. These adults, says Stephen Brand, won't be satisfied passing their retirement in front of the TV or sitting around talking about the good old days. Many have considerable expendable income and attach a high value to their time. These adults will be looking for compelling travel adventures and seeking involvement in their community and in the organizations they have supported throughout their adult lives.

Many nonworking adults want to fill their time with unique learning opportunities. The typical adult spends an average of five hundred hours a year in deliberate learning activities.[1] What is particularly different in the twenty-first century, however, is the abundance of American adults who are willing and able to pay others to enhance the quality of their lives. As business consultant Joseph Pine has noted,

People are working longer and harder and have more disposable income, which means that rather than relying on their own resources, they are more willing to pay somebody else to take care of their needs. We used to be responsible for all of our own services, like cooking, but now going out to eat is commonplace. We used to change the oil in our cars, and now we pay someone to do that. The entire history of economic progress is one of charging a fee for what once was free. In the same way, where we used to be responsible for our own experiences, we now pay other people to stage those experiences for us.[2]

When museum program planners plan and develop adult museum programs, they typically are not creating curriculum, but are designing meaningful experiences. Excellent learning experiences allow participants to observe closely or encounter something that is significant to them. The value of the experience in the end is personal, individually determined based on its internal impact.[3]

## Anatomy of an Adult Learner

*"Late again! Why is it that every evening I have something special to do, I end up having to stay late at work? And how many times have I told the kids to fill up the gas tank when it gets below a quarter tank? It took me five minutes in line before I could fill it tonight. Oh well, I should get to the museum just in time for the program.*

*"Oh no! The parking lot is full. Must be a big crowd. I'll have to find a spot on the street."*

*It took Jesse an extra seven minutes to find a parking spot and walk back to the museum entrance. He looked around for some announcement of where his program was being held, but saw none. Nor was there any orientation to the museum in general or guide to the building layout. The person at the front desk was busy talking to several visitors.*

*"I remember being in one of the rooms down that hall," he thought to himself. "I'll try that instead of stopping to ask and being even later."*

*But Jesse guessed wrong. He spent several more minutes trying other hallways before he heard a roar of laughter from a room. There was a note on the door identifying that room as the one in which his program was being held. He entered a packed auditorium. The only seats available were metal folding chairs. He parked his bulk on an empty chair and began to listen.*

*When Jesse had discussed the program with his wife, Sylvia, both had agreed that the program sounded interesting and worth attending. The museum had planned and marketed the program well. He spotted Sylvia down front with their neighbor, Ellie. They were still smiling at what must have been a pretty good story or joke. But Jesse just could not pick up the gist of what the speaker was saying. The terminology he was using and the concepts he was discussing were unfamiliar to Jesse. Try as he might, he just couldn't catch on to the ideas being expressed. He must have missed something important in those first twelve minutes.*

*In spite of the uncomfortable chair, Jesse stayed until the major presentation had concluded. Then he left. He knew there would be a question-and-answer or discussion period, but he felt anything he would say would just confirm how dumb he was. Sylvia could drive home with Ellie. Maybe he would come back next week for the second session in the series, but he doubted it.*

*Sylvia meanwhile was really enjoying the session. Dr. Kathrine Shea, the director of education, had been in the entryway, welcoming people to this special program. Sylvia also met some interesting people whose questions and comments made her feel confident that she had enough background knowledge to follow the speaker's ideas. She settled back into her seat to listen to the introduction. Dr. Shea did a good job of introducing the speaker and building a bridge between the presenter and the local group, giving the audience several reasons why they should listen to the ideas of the presenter. She also promised there would be time for questions and discussion after the talk.*

*The guest presenter started off with a bang. From the very beginning he used colorful terminology and vivid examples that made it easy to picture what he was talking about. He had delightful stories that related to the theme of the presentation. And more important to Sylvia, he set everyone at ease by explaining the concepts and terminology he would be using throughout the talk. "What a wonderful orientation," she had thought, feeling more and more at ease.*

*The speaker also used some great visuals to help the crowd understand and mentally picture the major points of the presentation. Throughout the presentation he asked questions instead of just giving answers to get the audience thinking.*

*The speaker posed a question to begin the discussion session. After a few people in the audience shared their ideas, he suggested all take a few minutes to talk to those around them and share their comments and questions. The place turned into a real buzz session. When the leader called the group back together again, the comments and insights shared by attendees were fascinating. Sylvia was so absorbed that she had not realized she was on her feet making a remark until she got positive feedback on her comment by some of those near her.*

*The session ended with a handout from the speaker providing a list of additional resources on the topic. The education director briefly described the next session of the program and invited everyone back with a promise of another interesting evening. Sylvia and Ellie definitely intended to return. But as they walked out Ellie said, "That certainly was enjoyable but I wonder how long we're going to remember anything we learned tonight?"*

Adult learning in museum programs is a very complex issue. In the above story Jesse had a very disappointing experience. His problems had little to do

with the program presenter or the content of the program. His work schedule, traffic and parking problems, and lack of familiarity with the museum
building led to his missing the introduction of the program and consequently
the introduction to the topic. Dr. Shea, the museum educator, followed many
recommended procedures, but did not account for latecomers in her plans.
The presenter was excellent, doing many of the things that make a good
adult educator. Sylvia and Ellie benefited and would return as excited adult
learners. But Ellie asked the all-important question: What had they really
learned? Had the program changed them in any way?

Adults order the world in a way that makes sense within the context of their
own experiences and culture. One key to developing programs capable of transforming adult participants lies in understanding mature learning interests and
needs. Adult learning expert Rosemary Caffarella summarizes the critical aspects of adult learning in this way:

- Adults want to learn, regardless of age.

- Adults have a rich background of knowledge and experience.
  They tend to learn best when their experience is acknowledged
  and new information builds on past knowledge and experience.
  (As Malcolm Knowles explains it, "experience is a resource for
  learning; when experience is ignored, adults perceive it as a rejection of themselves as a person.")[4]

- Both internal and external forces motivate adults to learn. It is
  important to understand the nature of these forces and how they
  interact to inhibit and encourage learning.

- All adults have preferred learning styles, and these differ from individual to individual.

- Adults are generally pragmatic and want to apply their learning to
  current situations.

- Adults come to a learning situation with personal goals and objectives, which may or may not be the same as those that underlie
  the learning situation.

- Adults prefer to be actively involved in the learning process rather
  than passive recipients of knowledge.

- Adults learn in both independent, self-reliant modes and in interdependent, connected, and collaborative ways. They want the opportunity to be supportive of each other in the learning process.

- The things adults learn tend to have an effect on others (for example, work colleagues or family members).

- Adults are more receptive to learning when they feel both physically and psychologically comfortable.

- What, how, and where adults learn is affected by gender, ethnicity, background, and the individual's many roles (for example, worker, parent, partner, friend, spouse).[5]

Basically, adults need and want to learn. They "engage in an educational activity because of some innate desire for developing new skills, acquiring new knowledge, improving already assimilated competencies, or sharpening powers of insight."[6] In museums, adults do so at their leisure.

## The Effect of Life Stages

Life stages have a significant effect on how adults spend their time, including whether or not they participate in voluntary learning activities. Typically, adults eighteen to thirty-five years old are busy establishing themselves in their work and home lives and their social and learning activities reflect these needs. Adults between the ages of thirty-five and fifty-five have generally established their basic family and professional relationships and are likely to show interest in "extracurricular" learning and community involvement. Adults age fifty-five and older show a pattern of interest in culture and their living memory as they enjoy new leisure time.

Angela Graham's study of museum learners revealed that middle-aged adult learners frequently pursue a subject in which they were interested between the ages of nine and twelve. Interests explored in childhood typically lie dormant during early adulthood, while unrelated degrees are earned and careers are advanced. Twenty or more years later, that interest resurfaces as the mature man or woman looks for connections between disciplines or seeks a "higher truth."[7]

*Adults explore an archaeological dig. (Photo by Bruce Selyem. Courtesy Museum of the Rockies.)*

## What Adults Choose to Learn

When asked to describe all of the areas in which they are conducting significant learning projects, "one that takes 10 or more hours," adults in the "Elder-learning Study" replied:

| Subject | (N=860) | Percent |
|---|---|---|
| music, art, dance, arts-related crafts | 505 | 58.7 |
| travel or travel related | 444 | 51.6 |
| literature, drama, humanities | 400 | 46.5 |
| politics, foreign affairs, current events | 316 | 36.7 |
| history, family history, genealogy | 314 | 36.5 |
| health and nutrition | 307 | 35.7 |
| philosophy, religion, self-actualization | 285 | 33.1 |
| computers, computer programs | 277 | 32.2 |
| finances, financial planning, investing | 250 | 29.1 |
| sports, leisure, recreation | 211 | 24.5 |
| nature, biological sciences | 210 | 24.4 |
| writing, journalism, journal keeping | 206 | 24.0 |
| gardening or agriculture | 191 | 22.2 |
| languages or multicultural learning | 162 | 18.8 |

| environment or environmental studies | 133 | 15.5 |
|---|---|---|
| field of current or previous career | 127 | 14.8 |
| physical sciences | 123 | 14.3 |
| community development | 95 | 11.0 |
| building construction, home repair | 94 | 10.9 |
| learning for a new career | 25 | 2.9 |

Source: Lois Lamdin, Elderlearning: New Frontier in an Aging Society (Phoenix: Oryx, 1997), 74.

## Motivations for Participating in Museum Programs

All adults are learners, even though many do not participate in organized museum programs. Better-educated adults with stable financial resources are more likely to participate in more formal adult education opportunities than other segments of the population.[8] The National Center for Education Statistics found that 50 percent of all adults in the United States participated in some type of formal learning activity in 1999. These learning activities included for-credit courses, work-related classes, and personal development experiences. Adults between the ages of eighteen and forty-four were more likely to take for-credit classes. Better-educated adults ages forty-four and older were more likely to participate in other types of activities, including those offered in museums. More women than men participated in these informal adult programs.[9]

The key to developing effective, attractive, and meaningful museum experiences for *all* adults lies in understanding adults' unique learning needs and preferences. What motivates adults to participate in new learning experiences? What are they learning and how? What keeps them coming back?

In our study, researchers discovered motivational differences between adult learners attending museum programs and adult learners in other informal learning environments.[10] In the broader population of adult learners, participants are usually motivated to enroll in a class because of a specific need (often related to employment) or the desire to develop a skill or create a product. While many museum programs cater to this type of learning, most of the museum program participants our team interviewed said they were taking classes on wreath making, Web-page design, or scientific illustration simply because they wanted to learn. These "knowledge seekers" were in the majority, although additional motivations emerged as well. Based on their primary motivation for participating, adult learners attending museum programs can be grouped into four general categories: knowledge seekers, socializers, skill builders, and museum lovers.[11]

**Why Do Adults Attend Learning Programs?**

A recent Elderlearning Study of Americans ages fifty-five and older asked respondents what motivated their participation in educational programs. The answers reflected an overwhelming desire to learn for "learning's sake."

| Responses | (N=860) | Percent |
|---|---|---|
| For the joy of learning | 685 | 79.7 |
| To pursue a long-standing interest or hobby | 498 | 57.9 |
| To meet people and socialize | 461 | 53.6 |
| To engage in creative activity | 406 | 47.2 |
| To pursue a new interest or hobby | 373 | 43.4 |
| To fill time productively | 343 | 40.0 |
| As part of a search for meaning and wisdom | 324 | 37.7 |
| To fill blanks in previous education | 214 | 24.9 |
| For community service | 182 | 21.2 |
| To help in present job | 40 | 4.7 |
| To prepare for new job or career | 21 | 2.4 |

Source: Lois Lamdin, *Elderlearning: New Frontier in an Aging Society* (Phoenix: Oryx, 1997), 75.

## Knowledge Seekers

*"I took the class because it was perfectly suited to my intellectual needs. I wanted to learn something new and I was very interested in the subject."*

Program participant, docent training

Knowledge seekers demonstrate a strong desire to learn new things. Not surprisingly, they form the largest subgroup of adult museum program participants. They seek challenging content, a broad array of learning activities, and additional resources that allow them to follow up on their interests.[12]

## Socializers

*"My daughter suggested that we take the class together."*

Program participant, natural history museum

Many adults attend museum programs expressly for social interaction. People new to an area often attend adult programs as a way to get to know people with similar interests. Typical socializers are family members, neighbors, or friends who attend programs together, using the outings as opportunities to spend time together.

Benefits go beyond simple socializing. People who may be too shy to ask questions in front of a group can quietly ask their companions for explanations. Perhaps most importantly, participants can share the experience after the program is over. Attending a program with another person makes the experience last. For example, a married couple taking an architecture class gains a new topic of conversation. And when traveling to a new city or seeing a new building, they can use what they learned to discuss what they see.

*"My housemate wanted to go to the program, and it sounded interesting, so I went along."*

Program participant, art museum

A small but interesting subset of the socializer category is the "tag-along." Many people attend a program because a spouse or friend is interested but doesn't want to go alone. "Come on," the instigator says, "it'll be fun." The social component is the driving force for tag-alongs, who may not have an active interest in the subject but will accompany others in order to spend time with them.

## Skill Builders

*"I'm opening a landscape design business and wanted to learn the tools of the trade."*

Program participant, natural history museum

Skill builders like to learn by doing. Their goal is to improve specific skills and gain new ones, and they want high-quality training. (We found significantly fewer skill builders than knowledge seekers among our interviewees.)

## Museum Lovers

*"I wanted to be involved with our museum because it is so dynamic."*

Program participant, art museum

This distinct group of adult museum program participants loves the museum and everything it stands for. Museum lovers make up the core audience for most adult programs, signing up for class after class after class. They often volunteer in several areas of the museum and know what programs will be offered even before calendars are distributed. They contribute financial support and are the museum's biggest fans, but they can also be an institution's sharpest critics.

## Adult Learning

Adults are accustomed to directing their own learning activities. Occasionally, they will engage in some formal learning activities in which the educational leader decides what aspects of the topic the group will learn and how the learning will occur, but adults usually choose informal approaches in which they control how they will learn. To get information, many adults read newspapers and magazines, talk to others, watch television, and surf the Internet. When attending more formal educational programs, they turn some of this control over to program leaders, though they still maintain independence.

One of the biggest differences between childhood and adult learning is the tremendous amount of experience adults have accumulated. As they grow into adulthood and need to respond independently to personal situations, adults rely more on their vast reservoir of experiences. Each individual constructs his or her reality. This is done within a social framework that has a great deal of influence on the interpretation of reality.

During the past two decades, much attention has been given to the learning styles and preferences of adults. Researchers have revealed that individuals' learning styles and preferences differ, and that these styles and preferences affect the success and satisfaction adults derive from new learning experiences. We also know that we can "learn how to learn" by improving our learning strategies.[13] Furthermore, brain research is beginning to give us hints on improving learning design and sharpening our self-directed learning attempts.

## Transformative Learning

Most of the new knowledge adults acquire is "additive" in that it builds on what is already known. But occasionally, new information or insight is so powerful it leads adults to reassess much of what they think they know. Jack Mezirow, a professor of adult education at Teachers College, Columbia University, has been a leader in describing transformative learning. In his book, *Transformative Dimensions of Adult Learning*, he explains:

> Normally, when we learn something, we attribute an old meaning to a new experience. In other words, we use our established expectations to explicate and

construe what we perceive to be the nature of a facet of experience that hitherto has lacked clarity or has been misinterpreted. In transformative learning, however, we reinterpret an old experience (or a new one) from a new set of expectations, thus giving a new meaning and perspective to the old experience.[14]

Breaking free to form new perspectives or outlooks on the world or our lives is truly "adult" learning, for it transforms our earlier conceptions of reality. Previously unexamined beliefs may be full of assumptions, contradictions, and prejudices. When adults encounter new information, insights, beliefs, and behaviors, they may be prompted to reinterpret past learning and experience. Given an opportunity to reflect on ingrained beliefs, adults may discover that prejudices are unjustified and that contradictions in their beliefs are a function of incomplete information. They develop new perspectives. This is often referred to as "meaning making" and is not always easy.

## Promoting Transformative Learning at the Science Museum of Minnesota

At the Science Museum of Minnesota, Vice President for Education David Chittenden promotes the following principles to encourage and support transformative learning:

- Learning demands trust
  *An atmosphere of trust is fundamental to the learning paradigm. By remaining open in our perspectives we maintain trust with our visitors.*

- Learning implies mutual respect and connections
  *We respect our visitors and the ideas, life experiences, feelings, and questions they bring with them. We seek to link science content, science concepts, and our visitors' lives in meaningful ways.*

- Learning is a personal journey
  *Because learning is an individual journey, we value and understand each visitor's uniqueness. At our best, we will stimulate interest that may motivate our visitors to continue their journey.*

- Learning is active
  *Learning is an active process, not a passive endeavor. Our programs and exhibits propel visitors from a passive to an active learner state—a state that involves both the emotions and the intellect, and that engages both the hand and the mind.*

*continued*

*continued*

- Learning is a social experience
  *While respecting the personal nature of all learning, we believe that learning experiences and positive learner outcomes are best mediated through social experiences and interactions.*

- Learning is a question-driven process
  *We believe that activities using inquiry and question-centered approaches enrich learning more than answer-centered approaches. The process, or "ways in which we know," is as important as the content of what we know.*

*Source:* Science Museum of Minnesota.

## Meaning Making

In her book *From Knowledge to Narrative*, Lisa Roberts distinguishes between a logical, scientific approach to understanding the world and a narrative approach that establishes not truth, but meaning in people's lives.[15] Roberts believes that meaning making lies at the very heart of the "museum enterprise" and especially serves those who attend programs for reasons of empowerment, experience, and ethics. Including multiple voices and views in programs is important to the meaning-making process. Roberts writes:

> To acknowledge that meaning making lies at the heart of the museum enterprise and that narrative provides the means by which this activity is accomplished is to take the first step toward truly opening museums to multiple voices and views. No one wants to throw "traditional" museums to the wind but rather to guide them toward more inclusive currents. This alone will enable museums to continue to fulfill their role as social institutions, in the truest sense of the term, in service to their communities.[16]

As noted in the introduction to this book, both Lisa Roberts and Jack Mezirow argue that the ultimate goal of learning is to help us make meaning in our lives or to transform our insight into some aspect of our knowledge base. The example was given of the participant who was able to integrate ideas from a botanic garden program into home landscaping. Given how adults learn, fostering meaning making and transformative adult learning seems to be an appropriate goal for adult museum programs. As David Carr states,

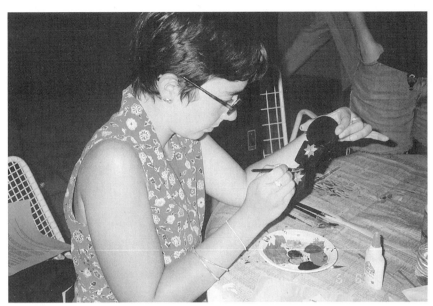

*Woman working on a straw appliqué piece after receiving background information and instruction in the northern New Mexican Hispanic folk tradition at the Museum of International Folk Art. This museum program was a collaboration with Project Sol out of Teachers College, Columbia University. (Courtesy Museum of International Folk Art.)*

The truths of individual lives are crafted truths, constructed from questions often asked out loud. Unlike any other structure in human society, the cultural institution is an ideal setting for public inquiry. Such dialogues need to happen in the presence of objects, and information, and other informed people.[17]

## Perspective Transformation

Perspective transformation is the process through which adults change their meaning schemes and meaning perspectives. Its importance lies in the obvious fact that, if we have not reflected in depth on our meaning schemes and perspectives, there are likely to be numerous contradictory, inadequate, and prejudicial elements within them. According to Mezirow, "Perspective transformation involves (a) an empowered sense of self, (b) more critical understanding of how one's social relationships and culture have shaped one's beliefs and feelings, and (c) more functional strategies and resources for taking action."[18]

Reflection upon assumptions and basic premises may convince adults that what has been taken for granted is unjustified. Progressive meaning perspectives tend to be more inclusive, holistic, and open. Adults tend to be more aware of assumptions and emotions and more critical of the stances taken in the past. This process is augmented by social interaction, which may provide support for change as well as for development of alternative perspectives.

## Adult Learner Outcomes

When our research team asked program participants if a particular program changed them in any way, their answers ranged from "No," to dramatic descriptions of life transformation. Even well-designed programs with excellent instructors, committed participants, intriguing content, and rich context won't have an impact on every individual. But because of the personal nature of transformative learning, all types of museum programs have the *potential* to effect change in participants. Some profound transformative effects are not always immediately perceived, understood, or fully realized. In fact, Michael Spock theorizes that learner outcomes may actually evolve over time. The impact of a program may be revealed to an individual gradually, after an opportunity for reflection or a new experience gives the program new meaning.[19]

Visualize the qualities or levels of informal adult learning as a pyramid. Our study findings show that the acquisition of skills and knowledge is the most common immediate outcome of adult learning in museums, while life-changing experiences stand at the pinnacle.

### Knowledge and Skill Acquisition

- Information expanded

- Interest in, or rejection of, new topic

- Knowledge expanded globally

- New knowledge or skills incorporated into life

- Follow-up materials obtained

When adults acquire and use new information, they are incorporating learning into their lives. As one program participant put it, "I've gone canoeing since taking this class, and now I hit fewer rocks." Not surprisingly, he deemed the program a success. Along with exercising new skills, participants in a successful program are likely to be open to new ideas, pursue further study, and obtain follow-up materials.

**Table 1.1.   Taxonomy of Learning Outcomes**

Life-Changing Experience

Transformed Perspective

Changed Attitude or Emotion

Increased Appreciation or Meaningfulness

Expanded Relationships

Knowledge and Skill Mastery

Expanded Relationships

- Developing community contacts
- Making new friends
- Sharing ideas with others

Expanded relationships include making new friends, developing community contacts, and sharing ideas with family, friends, and coworkers. As many participants said, "It's great to be with people of similar interests and enthusiasm."

Increased Appreciation or Meaningfulness

- Engaging in similar or follow-up learning experiences
- Discussing subject with knowledgeable individuals

- Reporting new insights or appreciation

- Increased awareness of social issues

Museum programs can offer avenues for reflection and foster deeper appreciation of the arts and sciences or community issues. A participant in an art class said, "Drawing gives me a sense of peace and relaxation and appreciation of life. It's a chance to step away from a busy life and appreciate the finer things." Developing new perspectives and greater appreciation are dramatic examples of ways museum programs can broaden horizons and open people's minds to new ideas.

In fact, many museum program participants felt inspired to pursue further study. Adult learners used museum programs to exercise underdeveloped talents and discover new ones. Many adults who initially had only a vague idea of what to expect from museum programs found them interesting, even transformative. When participants walk out of a program saying, "I will buy the supplies and keep going with it at home," they exhibit a measurable indicator of personal change.

### Changed Attitude or Emotion

- Heightened self-confidence

- Independent continued development

- Leading discussions or activities

- Pursuing activities on one's own

An important indicator of personal change is the willingness to engage in projects or activities that had previously been avoided. Self-confidence, emotional development, new attitudes, and spiritual and personal growth all can be measurable affective results of participation in a museum program. Frequently, grateful participants openly acknowledge such development, for instance, docents who cite newfound abilities to speak in public. Personal development also can be glimpsed in the continuing behavior of learners. They may engage in similar or follow-up learning experiences, as did the participant in one science camp who said, "The class definitely changed me. I am more likely to take on camping experiences now. . . . I have more confidence camping alone."

Other changed participants may go on to discuss relevant subjects with knowledgeable individuals and describe new insights or appreciation. Occasionally, such learners volunteer to help at the museum. Heightened social competence is also evidenced. Participants develop interpersonal relationships, promote cultural and community values, and demonstrate civic pride.

## Transformed Perspective

- Making new meaning in the participants' lives

- Greater acceptance of other ways of life

- Becoming more engaged with the museum

- Trusting in one's own creativity

- Speaking about the experience as a whole

- Accepting greater responsibility for social issues

Increased tolerance of others, trust in one's own creativity, and acceptance of greater responsibility for social issues all indicate that perspectives have been transformed and meaning making has taken place. These sorts of internal changes are revealed through such remarks as, "I never thought of it that way," or "I've never seen that before in this painting."

Frequently, such learners speak about their experience. Some become more engaged with the museum as a result. When participants describe gaining a greater worldview or a new set of connections and correlations between various dimensions of museum experiences, they are articulating an awakening to new ideas. Such transformations of perspective are meaning making.[20]

## Life-Changing Experience

- Making major changes in lifestyle

- Seeing things in a whole new way

- Developing a system for interpreting aspects of reality

- Contributing to efforts to change social patterns

- Giving back to community and helping others

Museum programs that inspire participants to change their lives are truly the epitome of transformative learning. A particularly powerful example comes from a docent at a natural history museum who told our team, "The docent program had a definite impact on me; I left physics. Astrophysics has taken a backstage to anthropology. It has opened up an entirely new world for me. The program changed how I spend my time. Before this I had never spent a second on life science." Such a statement clearly demonstrates the potential impact museum programs can have on participants.

Program participants who have had life-changing experiences may make major changes in their lifestyle that are quite evident to those around them. They may speak of seeing things in a whole new way or tell stories about new meaning in their lives. As one program participant said, "Floating the Grand Canyon was a life-altering experience. I realized that I had a place in the cosmos and was part of the timeless nature of the canyon." Some develop a system for interpreting aspects of reality or contribute to efforts to change social patterns.

## Effecting Change in Learners

All types of museum programs have the potential for creating excellent experiences and for effecting change in participants. This finding reflects the personal nature of transformative learning. Participants who are anticipating change and willing to be affected by museum educational programs are more likely to experience a personal event that includes positive change.

Change initially occurs from within an individual. The participants themselves must be open to new ideas before a program can affect them in any meaningful way. At the same time, poorly designed and executed programs may not have a positive lasting effect on any participants and, worse, a bad program might stifle a budding interest.

Personal change, or transformation, comes in a multitude of forms. The expectations that lectures impart knowledge, that classes build specific skills or a deeper understanding of a topic, and that longer-term field experiences cause more lasting impact seem reasonable; however, every type of program has the potential to produce a wide range of growth in its respective participants.

## Measuring Change

Museum visitors are likely to offer more information about their museum experience when queried about it at least six to eight weeks after their visit, instead of immediately after. This interim period gives visitors a chance to assess their experiences and apply them to their lives. In our survey, we allowed about this much time to elapse between museum programs and our interviews of participants. We found that evaluations and interviews conducted weeks after a museum program ended did indeed offer a better understanding of the program's impact.

Some of the more profound effects of program experiences are not always immediately perceived or understood. Often the impact of a program is revealed to an individual over a longer period of time. As time passes, some adults develop stronger emotional attachments to the experience as they reflect on it. This is more evidence that excellent museum programs can change adults in significant and lasting ways.

## Measuring Excellence in Museum Programs

At the root of *Adult Museum Programs: Designing Meaningful Experiences* are two basic premises. The first is that excellent museum programs deliver experiences, memorable events, and activities that engage individuals in very personal ways. The second premise is that transformation or change is a measure of an excellent experience. The extent to which museum programs are successful can indeed be measured by their ability to affect, inform, empower, and change people and, in doing so, help them improve themselves.

This emphasis on transformation does not in any way negate the importance of the acquisition of new knowledge or skills that so frequently occurs in museums and other places. Rather, as museums have the capacity to transform adults' insights into meaningful aspects of life, museums should reach toward that possibility. Chapter 2 examines the various types of museum programs that can serve the diverse needs of independent and active adult learners.

## Notes

1. Alan Tough, *The Adult's Learning Projects* (Toronto: Ontario Institute for Studies in Education, 1971).

2. B. Joseph Pine, "Interview: B. Joseph Pine—Experience Required," interview by Meridith Levinson, *CIO Magazine*, November 15, 1999, 3.

3. Pine, "Interview," 3.

4. Malcolm Knowles, *The Adult Learner: A Neglected Species* (Houston: Gulf, 1973), 75.

5. Rosemary Caffarella, *Planning Programs for Adult Learners* (San Francisco: Jossey-Bass, 1994).

6. Stephen Brookfield, *Understanding and Facilitating Adult Learning* (San Francisco: Jossey-Bass, 1986), 11.

7. Angela Graham, "Persistence without External Rewards: A Study of Adult Learners in Art Museum and Planetarium Education Programs" (Ph.D. diss., Northern Illinois University, 1990).

8. Carol Aslanian and Henry Brickell, *Americans in Transition: Life Changes as Reasons for Adult Learning* (New York: College Entrance Examination Board, 1980).

9. *The Condition of Education 2000* (Washington, D.C.: National Center for Education Statistics, 2000), 10.

10. Sharon Merriam and Rosemary Caffarella, *Learning in Adulthood* (San Francisco: Jossey-Bass, 1991), 80–83.

11. This categorization fits well with the long-accepted research published by Cyril Houle in *The Inquiring Mind* (1962). Through a series of interviews, Houle concluded that there were three major orientations to learning among adults. Though challenged often, this categorization is still honored by the general field of adult education. Houle acknowledged that there were "learning-oriented" participants who, like our knowledge seekers, seek knowledge for knowledge's sake. He labeled another group "goal-oriented" learners, for they used the educational program to pursue some specific goal, much the same as our skill builders do. His final class, "activity-oriented" learners who seek learning activities especially for social interaction, is similar to our socializers. As with most organizations, museums develop a clientele very loyal to their institution. These may be members of any of Houle's three categories, but their primary orientation is to all the learning activities of their museum.

12. Not all respondents indicated that they were at a museum program solely to expand their horizons. Instead, we found that some program participants wanted to gain a particular skill, that they attended for social reasons, or that they just loved the museum and went to everything they could. So it is important to note that none of these categories are completely exclusive. Most adults attend museum programs for myriad reasons. They not only may be interested in the subject and want to learn more about it, but they may also want to spend time with their friend who is also attending the activity or to bring home something they produced in a class.

13. Robert Fellenz and Gary Conti, "Learning and Reality: Reflections on Trends in Adult Learning," in *ERIC Clearinghouse on Adult, Career, and Vocational Education*, 7–11 (Columbus: Ohio State University, 1989).

14. Jack Mezirow, *Transformative Dimensions of Adult Learning* (San Francisco: Jossey-Bass, 1991), 8.

15. Lisa Roberts, *From Knowledge to Narrative: Educators and the Changing Museum* (Washington, D.C.: Smithsonian Institution Press, 1998), 134.

16. Roberts, *From Knowledge to Narrative*, 152.

17. David Carr, "The Adult Learner in the Museum," in *Museums and Universities: New Paths for Continuing Education*, ed. J. W. Solinger (New York: Collier Macmillan, 1990).

18. Mezirow, *Transformative Dimensions*, 8.

19. Hope Leichter and Michael Spock, "Learning from Ourselves: Pivotal Stories of Museum Professionals," in *Bridges to Understanding Children's Museums* (Cleveland: Case Western Reserve University, 1999), 41; Michael Spock, "The Stories We Tell about Meaning Making," *Exhibitionist* 18, no. 2 (1999): 32.

20. Roberts, *From Knowledge to Narrative*, 152.

# CHAPTER TWO

# SOUL-SEARCHES TO SOCIALS: TYPES OF MUSEUM PROGRAMS FOR ADULT LEARNERS

A good museum program gets someone to the "Ahhh" moment—to a new way of looking at things.

—Guy Kaulukukui, chairman of the Education Department at the Bishop Museum

Inspiration for program ideas can be found just about anywhere, from permanent exhibits and special collections to current events and community celebrations. Settling on a program topic or theme is just the first step—a great topic does not guarantee a great program. Choosing the right approach or format in which to present your ideas establishes a firm foundation for building excellent program experiences.

In our research, we observed many types of programs. Some were strengthened by collaboration with other institutions or organizations. Others used wine-and-cheese receptions to encourage social interaction and dialogue. Many museums serve themselves while they serve others through docent training programs. More and more institutions are expanding the traditional scope of museum programs as they whisk people off to faraway places to study exotic flora, fauna, and culture. Other museums are using programs to touch people's hearts as well as their minds.

## Bread-and-Butter Programs

The most common kinds of programs currently being offered by all types of museums are volunteer and docent training, lectures, and guided tours. In addition to these staples, science-based museums frequently offer field trips, gallery demonstrations, and workshops, while art- or history-based museums might be more likely to offer performing arts events, symposia, and film series. But in fact, we observed all program types at all categories of museums, with the exception of field schools, which we saw only at science-based museums.

**Table 2.1.    Top Three Types of Programs Offered at Both Science- and Art/History-Based Museums**

|  | Science Museums | Art/History Museums |
|---|---|---|
|  | (percent of museums surveyed offering the program) | |
| Volunteer/Docent Training | 94% | 95% |
| Lectures | 86% | 86% |
| Guided Tours | 82% | 84% |

**Table 2.2.    Popular Types of Programs Offered at Science-Based Museums**

|  | Science Museums |
|---|---|
| Field Trips | 75% |
| Gallery Demonstrations | 72% |
| Workshops | 72% |

**Table 2.3.    Popular Types of Programs Offered by Art- and History-Based Museums**

|  | Art and History Museums |
|---|---|
| Performing Arts | 75% |
| Symposia | 63% |
| Film Series | 53% |

## Factors That Determine the Type of Program Offered

Our project team discovered that the type of program offered for adults depends on many factors, including:

- The museum's mission.

- The program planner's ability to share guidelines and concerns with instructors, and his or her understanding of the essentials of successful program planning.

- The size of the audience. (Some programs, such as lectures, gallery demonstrations, gallery talks, symposia, and dramatic performances, are better suited for large audiences. Others, such as tours, field trips, seminars, gallery demonstrations, hands-on workshops, informal discussions, and short courses, are appropriate for small audiences.)

- The audience's needs, preferences, and learning styles.

- The facility available.

- The material presented, including access to collections.

- The instructor's experience with various teaching strategies, such as facilitating discussion, generating hands-on activities, and engaging in question-and-answer sessions.

- The tradition of the institution.

- The budget.

## A Sampler of Program Types

The following sampler of program formats shows the tremendous variety and scope of approaches available to program planners. While there is an inventory of stock program formats from which to choose, innovative program planners are open to creating "hybrid" approaches to meet specific needs in various learning situations.

### Lectures

Lectures are among the most common types of adult programs offered in museums. They are easy to plan, economical to run, and can efficiently meet the museum's educational mission by presenting relevant material to large numbers of adults over a short period of time. Over 90 percent of the museums we interviewed offered lectures for adults.

Lectures are well-prepared presentations about selected objects or subjects given by a qualified docent, curator, or instructor. "Qualified" implies expertise in both content and presentation. Lectures may be stand-alone events, but are often more attractive when offered within a package of programs presenting varied views or insights on a particular topic.

As learning opportunities, lectures are limited by several factors: they offer a single point of view, the speaker may use language not suitable to the audience's background, and little interaction or active learning occurs. While highly educated individuals are accustomed to lectures and accept the format, other adult audiences are easily turned off by formal lectures.

Lectures or presentations can be improved simply by adding more presenters or more visual or auditory media. Presentations developed for television rarely feature only one person. Instead, producers put together panels, interviews, or group discussions, enlivened by a moderator. The moderator's role is critical, as he or she controls the process, making the whole presentation more active and ensuring balance among the speakers. Audiences enjoy the interaction among panelists and become engaged themselves as they choose panelists with whom to identify. To be truly successful, a lecture must allow time for questions or discussion. The program participants we interviewed repeatedly pleaded for time to question presenters.

Among the successful lecture programs we observed was the Florida Museum of Natural History's Senior Discovery Series, in which seniors enjoyed an informal lecture on paleontology. Participants brought bag lunches, while the museum provided beverages and dessert. The presence of refreshments encouraged social interaction and allowed for an informal discussion afterward.

At the Smithsonian Institution's National Gallery of Art, Friday evening lecturers introduce a provocative idea in thirty minutes, followed by a reception that allows participants to discuss ideas. The combination of food, a relaxed atmosphere, and the opportunity to reflect, share ideas, and meet people has proven to be a good one. The National Zoological Park in Washington, D.C., offers a similar program. Each of its "TGIF" lectures, accompanied by refreshments, are offered in a different animal house so that adults can observe the animals and ask questions while an animal keeper is talking.

Former executive director of Reynolda House Museum Nicholas B. Bragg shared with us his five rules for a successful lecture: (1) recognize that the audience is very general, (2) provide handouts, (3) never talk more than forty-five minutes without a break, (4) make time for discussion and questions, and (5) always relate the topic to the museum and its collections. Bragg added that the classroom should be a beehive of activity.

*Tips for Improving Lectures*

- Carefully choose speakers who can adjust their presentation to the knowledge and interest level of their audience.

- Have a museum staff member serve as an event host and moderator.

- Prepare and deliver a thoughtful introduction to the speaker and topic that illuminates links to the museum's overall program.

- Encourage speakers to emphasize no more than five or six points, use humor, tell stories, and give examples to keep the program varied and enjoyable.

- Encourage the use of audiovisual aids for clarity and to serve visually oriented learners.

- Encourage the lecturer to provide handouts, guidelines, references, or other follow-up resources for participants and to offer help to put them together.

- Organize and moderate a question-and-answer or discussion session involving participants.

Can lectures promote perspective transformation? Absolutely. Many adults constantly seek new insights from lectures. Others are inspired by the excitement that radiates from dynamic speakers who embody passion and vision. A series of good lectures can also encourage adults to return soon, thus creating sustained and deep relationships with the museum.

## Guided Tours in the Museum

*The elderly man at the information stand suggested I take a guided tour of a featured display of locally owned art. "The tour is scheduled to start in a few minutes and you could just join the group that is assembling in the third-floor gallery." I agreed and joined a small group waiting for a scheduled docent tour to begin.*

*The dominant piece in the area was a huge abstract painting with big blocky panels of red and yellow separated horizontally by a bold, black streak.*

*"Who in the world would have something like that in their house?" asked the woman standing next to me. She was about fifty years old and dominated in every way the man standing next to her. I presumed he was her husband.*

*He said, "I think that's a Rothko. Do you realize how much it's worth?"*

*"I don't care what it's worth! You couldn't pay me to have something like that in my house," she replied. Comments came from several of the bystanders—some curious, some comical, some critical. Much shaking of heads ensued.*

*After a bit of this banter, a woman who had been standing quietly in the rear of the group began speaking. "I'm the docent scheduled to lead this tour," she said. "Let's start by considering that painting you have been talking about."*

*"In what kind of room might you hang that painting?" she asked. A big room we all agreed. "But what style room? Victorian? Colonial?"*

*"I don't know," whispered a woman, "but it sure wouldn't match my couch."*

*"No, it wouldn't match my house either," replied the docent, "but if I owned a postmodern villa along the coast. . . ."*

*"Hmmm," we all muttered.*

*Next she asked, "Could you display it vertically instead of horizontally?" We all bent our heads to consider this bizarre perspective. One question after another flowed to the group. "What effect does the black horizontal line have?" "Could it be thicker?" "Thinner?" "A different color?" "What if the colors were reversed?"*

*The docent pulled out a color chart, giving us an opportunity to experience how colors affect our emotions. "What sort of emotion does this piece elicit from you?" As the group's responses became more thoughtful, she began slipping in little pieces of information about the painting and its creator. By the time she invited the group to move on, she had given us all a valuable lesson in how to examine and appreciate a piece of art.*

The guided tour is one of the most distinctive, long-standing educational programs offered by American museums. Nearly 88 percent of the museums we interviewed offered them. A guided tour is usually conducted by a staff member, docent, or volunteer and can be a brief overview of the entire museum or a more intensive tour of a main gallery, exhibit hall, or special exhibit. Depending on the tour leader's teaching style and the number of visitors involved, the tour format may be a lecture or an interactive discovery/inquiry session involving the visitors. The docent's teaching style and the content selected are critical factors in a tour's success.

Tours are challenging because a single group can include adults who joined the tour because they are interested in and informed about the content and adults who joined because they know nothing about the subject. The tours our researchers participated in lasted from fifteen minutes to nearly two hours and the number of participants varied widely. All this points up the fact that leaders must be responsive to many variables in order to conduct a successful tour.

Of course, tour leaders need to be knowledgeable guides. Visitors might ask questions about anything from the subject at hand, to general questions about the museum, to where they should go for dinner. But the docent's ability to relate to members of the group can be at least as important as what they know about their subject. The best tour leaders were not walking lecturers providing encyclopedic information on the content, but were friendly discussion leaders sharing what the subject of the tour meant to them. They also inquired into the interest and insights of the group and allowed time for participants to talk together.

The orientation provided at the beginning of a tour is very important and sets the tone for the entire experience. Adults usually want to know something about their guide. They also appreciate an overview of what they will hear, see, and experience. Rule-oriented participants want to know if they can ask questions, drop out of the group for a time, or record parts of the tour. Some want to know with whom they are touring, while others prefer to remain anonymous.

Distractions are inevitable. Noise from other visitors or from aspects of the tour itself can be irritating. Some distractions can be minimized by gathering groups into less noisy nooks. Such spots are even more valuable when they provide opportunities to sit and have a short discussion. Disturbance can also occur when people leave or join the touring group; adults are self-directed learners who pursue their own interests. Tour leaders need to accept this and not be bothered when it occurs; it is seldom a reflection on their performance.

Too often, tours are available only for organized groups that request a guide in advance. Individual museum-goers may seldom have an opportunity to participate in a museum tour. Providing regularly scheduled gallery tours or making guides available for adults who want to study a specific gallery or exhibit with a guide makes sense. At the Boise Art Museum, for example, docents lead drop-in tours of featured exhibits on the first and third Thursdays of each month. The Minneapolis Institute of Arts offered "serial" tours that look in-depth at various parts of their collection over a series of visits.

Some innovative gallery talks and tours use an "artful evening" approach, which may include music, food, and drink. The Josyln Art Museum's Appetite for Art is held the third Thursday evening of every month. The program offers a light sampling of thematic food and drink in conjunction with an insightful gallery talk on a special exhibition or an aspect of the permanent collection.

On a similar note are the popular Historic Alexandria Candlelight tours. These festive tours invite adults to explore five historic homes decorated for the holidays.

*Tips for Guided Tours*

- Train docents to take the time at the beginning of a tour to introduce themselves and encourage other adults in the group to do the same.

- Have docents take a minute to find out what the members of their group are the most interested in and build upon that interest.

- Limit group size to facilitate personal interaction or assign assistant guides to accompany larger groups.

- Coach docents on how to elicit individual ideas and reflections on objects.

- Do not require adults to participate in a tour. Let docents know it is all right if a member of a group wanders away to explore or if new adults join the original group.

- Help docents be prepared to answer questions and show them how to avoid letting one individual dictate the focus of the group.

- Train docents to respond to questions they do not know the answer to. Let docents know it is all right not to know the answer for every question.

Can guided tours lead to perspective transformation? Certainly. Below is a personal example from a researcher's observation notes.

*It was simply a gallery tour, "Highlights of the Museum," scheduled to last forty-five minutes or so. The leader was a middle-aged woman who had conducted this tour many times. There were seven tour members: a college-age couple from a rural area, a mother and twelve-year-old son from the city, one of our project staff members and his wife, and a lone seventy-plus-year-old man who walked with a cane. Yet it was one of the most memorable museum programs I ever experienced.*

*What made this tour an excellent museum program? It was well designed, with an exceptional leader, interested participants, and strong content situated in an engaging environment. The tour had clearly been planned to accommodate individuals' interests. The leader was experienced, knowledgeable, flexible, and related well to the participants. The people were complete strangers to all except their partners, yet they were open to sharing and learning from one another. The young couple noticed the difficulty the lone man had walking and arranged to push him in a wheelchair. The content selected by the leader was well suited to the group and was enhanced by unusual objects and beautiful dioramas. Several times the leader checked with the participants as to their interests. The tour was made even more pleasant because she guided us to quiet corners in the busy museum where we could sit, rest, and converse.*

*The tour guide was so amazed at the way the group bonded that she asked if we were all related. The result was that the learning process did not end when the tour concluded. We stayed together as a group for an additional half hour, sharing not just our impression of the museum, but also our life experiences and hopes for the future. The elderly man had directed communications in the Kennedy White House. The mother was using the museum to homeschool her son. The young couple was investigating the potential of dedicating their life to the ministry. And we were there to study what constitutes an excellent museum program! The sincerity of the young and the continuing dedication of the elderly revised my insight into the role of museum programs.*

## Docent Training

Docents are a vital part of museum education. Docent training is critical because the docent may be the only museum representative with whom visitors interact, apart from the person who collects their admission fee. It is the image of this docent that visitors carry away from the museum and that may determine whether or not they return. Museum educators and curators typically conduct these programs, however some institutions may use outside lecturers or local university faculty. According to our research, 93 percent of museums offer volunteer training, by far the most common adult education program in museums.

Docent training can take many forms and follow many different approaches. Some docent-training programs emphasize personal development, while others focus on content. Some programs are quite structured, while others are more flexible and rely on docents to be self-directed learners. However, the overarching objective is to educate docents about the museum's collections and train them in the best ways of presenting that material to the public.

Many of the best training programs we observed were quite extensive and included extended staff coaching. The docent-training program at the Carnegie Museum of Natural History takes three years to complete. New volunteers at the Museum of Science, Boston, work through a study packet at their own pace and regularly meet with a supervisor or trainer. Weekly training sessions last from thirty minutes to an hour. Discussion topics cover a wide range of current issues and events related to the particular area in which the docents work. The volunteer supervisor personally conducts new-volunteer orientation, on a one-to-one basis.

At the Museum of the Rockies, docent-training sessions run twice a week throughout the fall. The classroom is comfortable, with round tables that encourage interaction. Much of the learning is expected to occur outside of the classroom through readings and observation of other docent tours. Outstanding speakers are brought in from various departments of the museum and from outside sources. The museum maintains a well-stocked library and offers occasional trips to relevant sites outside the facility. Many docents participate in the program year after year to keep up to date on the latest discoveries in natural history and to improve their teaching skills. These extended relationships over a period of years are key ingredients for personal transformation.

If you have limited staff and resources, consider combining some docent and teacher training programs. The McNay Art Museum in San Antonio once offered a minicourse, "Low-Fat Art History," that consisted of a series of eight evening programs surveying art through history. The program was offered to both teachers and docents-in-training and participants could receive twelve hours of graduate credit for completing the course.

*Tips for Docent- and Volunteer-Training Programs*

- Offer personalized training programs whenever possible to fit an individual's experience and skills.

- Provide docents ongoing and consistent feedback as their learning coach and cheerleader.

- Provide excellent training materials, teaching resources, and equipment.

- Model effective teaching techniques for adults in exhibit galleries using teaching materials that are available to them.

- Create a docent-run advisory board to shape training programs and invite feedback from volunteers.

- Publicly recognize and reward docents for their service. Offer stickers, pins, plaques, or books as tangible rewards.

**CASE STUDY 2.1**

*Docent Discovery Training, Reynolda House Museum of American Art, Winston-Salem, North Carolina*

**General Description**

This introductory program to the Reynolda House collection correlates art with literature and music. After completing the program, docents lead tours for school groups and adults and become actively involved in family days, library research, flower arranging, and other duties and events. Training is offered in the fall and spring. Nine sessions are held on Wednesdays and Fridays from 9:30 A.M. to noon. Cost is $15 and includes the Reynolda House catalog.

**Institutional Perspective**

The arts are powerful conveyers of meaning and adults need to be reminded to relate their life experiences to art.

The Reynolda House has a unique approach in that all museum volunteers receive the same training and are called "docents." Some lead tours, some work in the library, some arrange flowers. There is no difference between a regular volunteer and a docent.

Two promises guide the docent-training program at Reynolda House: docents will always learn something and they will always be personally thanked. The training process reflects the respectful, personal process docents are expected to use with visitors. Docents are trained to encourage learning by raising questions rather than giving answers.

**Instructor's Perspective**

My goal in teaching the Docent Discovery Training class is to help participants understand the big picture. A compilation of arts from a particular historical era can tell us much of that period. Thus, this program combines music and art with some history.

My personal goal in teaching is to see the world through new eyes. I am very enthusiastic about the topic (the correlation between art, literature, and music) and believe that my enthusiasm will make an audience enthusiastic. I consider myself fairly methodical in my teaching style and use lectures and handouts. But I also am fairly "theatrical" and will dress in period costume. I like "to stage the scene."

I realize the audience is quite varied for museum programs, however I don't really deal with the variety. I feel it is better to present the subject well and let the participants adjust to the content.

*continued*

**CASE STUDY 2.1 (continued)**

**Participants' Perspectives**

1. Sue
Age: sixty-five
Education: postgraduate degree
Occupation: nurse

I signed up for the Docent Discovery class to develop a deeper knowledge of art and artists and make a greater personal connection to the museum by learning about its exhibits and collections. One of the most memorable aspects of the training was an activity that involved standing in front of paintings and thinking about how the art work affected my emotions.

I really liked the opportunity to choose my own area of interest within the docent-training program. Each student got to choose an artist, writer, and musician to study. I also liked being given time and access to the library for personal research.

I would like to see more lectures and films about artists whose work is in the museum and I'd like to see more programs that suggest correlations between art, music, literature, and history. Programs like that help put art into perspective.

I'm now much more involved in the museum. I visit the museum more often, give tours, volunteer in other areas of the museum, and bring more friends and relatives to the museum.

2. Eleanor
Age: sixty-five
Education: college graduate
Occupation: retired

I wanted to be involved with Reynolda House because it is so dynamic and is always offering so many different activities. I'm interested in art and many of the other activities of Reynolda House and I wanted to give tours for students.

The instructors challenged participants to think and discover things on their own. We were also challenged to think about our feelings and share our opinions and emotions with other participants.

I liked so many things about the class. It had a very mature, adult nature, and we weren't spoken down to or treated like children. Our opinions and feelings were encouraged and respected. The class was very challenging, with in-depth teaching and learning. I didn't much like the intensive nature of the class, though. We met twice a week for three hours each time. I wish it had been spread out a bit more.

The program gave me a new perspective on art and I have more interest in American art now because of this program. I'm also now a docent at the museum and I give tours for school groups. I use my new knowledge to challenge students to think about their emotions and to put art into a larger perspective.

## 3. Greg
Age: sixty
Education: postgraduate degree
Occupation: CPA and college instructor

I've been interested in art for many years and have visited many art museums and other museums all over the world. My wife has been a docent at the museum for years and I've been interested in taking part in docent training, too, because of her. I hoped to have the pleasure of being able to share my experiences with other people and to help them understand what the artists were trying to portray in their work.

I liked the way the training program correlated music, art, and literature. It was a great way to learn. I'll remember what I learned about art techniques and art in general. I'll particularly remember the artist I focused on and the correlations between art, literature, and music. And of course I'll remember the people in the class. I liked hearing other people's views and being able to express my own.

## 4. Rose
Age: forty-four
Education: high-school graduate
Occupation: homemaker

The reputation of Reynolda House is excellent. A friend took the class and loved it and suggested that I take the class, too. I hoped to gain some insight into American art, because I didn't have much previous knowledge in that field. I've long been interested in art, but didn't realize the extent and variety of the Reynolda House collection. Now I'm falling in love with American art.

I most remember doing a "Reflections" exercise in which I had to write ten lines about something that meant the most to me that day. I was impressed by the amount of sharing of information and ideas between instructors and docents. Everyone tried to help everyone else. The instructors put an emphasis on everyone helping each other. I also remember the correlations drawn between art, literature, and music. The hands-on activities in creating art forged good interaction between participants and helped develop a greater appreciation for abstract art.

*continued*

CASE STUDY 2.1 (*continued*)

### Research Observation

The training began with an introductory meeting over coffee. Participants sat in a circle and discussed why they wanted to be docents. They called this "leveling the playing field." This spirit was continued throughout the training period by starting each session with personal reflections.

At the conclusion of the course, docent trainees gave presentations to their classmates. Each trainee selected a painting from the Reynolda House collection, a piece of music, and a piece of literature, all from the same era. As they had been learning to do in the Docent Discovery program, the docents noted correlations between the art, music, and literature of a particular era. Some of the presenters played musical samples on a stereo, some read from period literature.

The best presentations used a multimedia approach and prompted the audience to really think about what they were seeing and hearing to create their own mental images of the era: "Imagine how it felt to . . . ," "Imagine what it was like to come home to . . . ," "Imagine how the artist felt when . . . ," "Imagine what this woman was thinking as she. . . ." The most effective presenters were able to weave for their audience a web of connections between artist, painting, music, and literature.

A brief discussion period followed each presentation. This allowed other docents to describe their thoughts and feelings about the works presented. One docent said something to the effect of, "I've looked at that Grant Wood landscape a hundred times and had never seen its sexuality. Now I wonder how I missed it." Insights from fellow trainees helped presenters learn what types of reactions they might get from museum visitors.

Docents interviewed about the training process were universally high in their praise of the program. Perhaps some of this is due to the way they were treated. Docents are given appreciation dinners (not potlucks) and the staff always thanks them personally. No one is scheduled for a task until they are contacted regarding the time and place.

### Analysis

Rather than dwelling on brush strokes, the Docent Discovery program uses a holistic approach to learning about art that fosters a broad understanding of art rather than a narrow interpretation of individual pieces. Such an approach offers excellent learning opportunities and marks this program as something truly special. The most important aspect of this program is its commitment to creating a bigger picture through the correlation between an era's music, literature, history, and art. Docents who graduate from this training have the experience and background to converse on a variety of topics rather than simply repeating facts heard in a lecture.

The first two participants are what we call "museum lovers" (introduced in chapter 1), who love what the museum offers and what it stands for. Generally, museum lovers are the core audience for all museum programs, including lectures, classes, field trips, travel programs, and especially docent-training programs.

The third participant is more difficult to characterize. He says he loves museums, so qualifies as a museum lover, but since his wife's involvement drew him into participation in the docent program, he also qualifies for the "tagalong" category of adult museum program participants. This illustrates the difficulty in attempting to pigeonhole museum program participants.

The fourth participant is not typical, because the vast majority of adult museum program participants are college educated. Yet adults without college degrees can be an important audience for the museum. How can museums persuade more people like this woman to become involved with the museum? In this case, a past participant marketed the program. As is pointed out in chapter 6, word of mouth is an extremely effective way of reaching audiences.

Despite the fact that many docent trainees can be categorized as museum lovers, it is important to note that they will still have individually different learning styles and preferences. One participant we spoke with thought the program was too "touchy-feely" in that she had to share personal feelings with other people. Other participants, however, found the emotional sharing exercises to be rewarding. Successful program planners need to keep this disparity in mind, despite the perception that all museum lovers share common values and preferences.

Overall, the Docent Discovery class had an enormous impact on participants. Many said that the docent-training program changed their perspective on art and that their involvement in the museum had increased dramatically. Such an experience is by no means exclusive to this museum. Docent-training programs at museums across the country serve as the primary tool for recruiting new and dedicated museum boosters.

## Field Trips

Instead of people coming *to* the museum on a field trip, program participants sally forth *from* the museum on learning adventures.

Field trips have become one of the more popular adult museum programs; 67 percent of the museums we interviewed offered them. These programs enable small groups of adults to socialize while actively experiencing the cultural and natural world. They differ from travel programs in duration, cost, and extent of content covered. While field trips may not necessarily relate to a museum's exhibits or collections, they are generally connected with the museum's mission.

Offered in a variety of formats, field trips might include anything from tours of other institutions to nature hikes, and take place at another site or while in transit.

In the Science Museum of Minnesota's Organ Crawl series, adults traveled to various churches throughout the Minneapolis-St. Paul area to see, hear, and even play various types of organs. In addition, they visited an organ factory to see how the instruments were made. Organ players and manufacturers led tours (see case study 3.1, on page 66).

*Tips for Conducting Field Trips*

- Recruit trip leaders who are knowledgeable, articulate, and personable.

- Ensure that trip leaders and program managers visit the site prior to the actual field trip so they are familiar with facilities and can learn of any accessibility issues or other problems ahead of time.

- Provide trip leaders with appropriate background information and teaching materials so they can make connections to the overall museum program.

- Always have a staff person participate as an event host.

- Provide name tags and encourage the field trip leader to start the trip with a group icebreaker.

- Use comfortable transit vehicles with restrooms whenever possible, especially for programs aimed at older adults.

- Actively involve participants while in transit. Ask them about their interests, tell a story, or conduct get-acquainted activities. Field-trip participants often have much to offer each other and the socializing adds to the enjoyment of the trip.

- Anticipate how much help will be required to serve beverages and food, coordinate logistics, or assist special-needs participants, and have adequate staff or volunteer help on hand.

- Plan trips far enough in advance so that every detail can be worked out and participants can be accurately informed of what to expect.

- Provide advance information about the trip on the museum's Web site.

- Create a field trip advance organizer and follow-up reading list for participants.

Well-planned field trips have a special capacity of placing adults in new, unfamiliar or disorienting environments. These moments can awaken child-like exploration and enthusiasm for the world. They can also trigger life-changing experiences.

### Gallery Demonstrations

Gallery demonstrations are presentations given within a museum gallery or exhibition hall and may or may not be directly related to an exhibit. They are generally open to all visitors, regardless of age. These programs allow visitors to see, for example, how an ancient tool was used or a Native American rug is woven. Some programs even provide a hands-on learning experience by allowing observers to try the activity themselves. Gallery demonstrations are great attention getters and sustain adult interest.

The Buffalo Bill Historical Center offers outstanding demonstrations on a daily basis through their summer artists-in-residence program. Artists are situated in various galleries and exhibition halls to demonstrate their crafts. Visitors are encouraged to watch, ask questions, and take handouts or other materials.

*Tips for Gallery Demonstrations*

- Demonstration leaders should practice their program ahead of time.

- Style the demonstrations more as conversation than lecture.

- Allow participants to take part in the demonstration, if possible.

- Ensure the demonstration can be seen by all viewers.

- Provide an opportunity for observers to ask questions.

*Bessie Theodorou demonstrates the preparation of a classic Greek dish.* (Courtesy Missouri Botanical Garden.)

Can demonstrations and gallery talks leave indelible impressions? Certainly. The personal attention and sharing of individual experiences can inspire and awaken adults to other realities.

## Teacher Workshops

Many museums offer some type of teacher-training program. This attests to the strong ties that exist between museums and schools and to the benefits of using museum resources in classrooms. Eighty percent of the museums in our survey offered teacher training. Programs may include weekend courses, one-day workshops, or one- to three-day conferences. Most programs offer teacher certification or graduate credit.

Workshops are action oriented. They bring people together to accomplish something specific and call for careful planning and efficient involvement of participants. Because they often involve a sizable group of people, workshops are often led by teams of people rather than by individuals.

The Smithsonian Institution's National Gallery of Art in Washington, D.C., offers a six-day interdisciplinary course for both teachers and administrators. The summer Teacher Institute is designed to meet both personal and professional enrichment needs. Courses address a central topic, bringing

*Basket making during a teacher symposium put on by the Autry Museum of Western Heritage with the Los Angeles Zoo and the Satwiwa Native American Cultural Center, Santa Monica Mountains, called "Climate, Creatures, and Cultures of the Los Angeles Basin."* (Courtesy Autry Museum of Western Heritage.)

together educators from across the country to study, reflect, and learn with colleagues. Institute topics have included American art, impressionism, European Renaissance, early modernism, and mythology.

The Chula Vista Nature Center, in Chula Vista, California, has devised a novel approach to teacher training. Their "Field Trip Orientation Workshops" are designed to give teachers and group leaders the materials and information necessary to lead a successful Nature Center field trip. Elementary-aged children are not allowed to tour the center unless their teacher or group leader has taken the three-hour workshop. These trainees become the museum's "master teachers" and are notified of upcoming workshops when new curriculum is developed or when exhibits change. Their master teacher card allows them free admission to the center and a 10 percent discount in the gift shop. According to the Chula Vista Nature Center, this program has alleviated docent burnout. In addition, unprepared teachers and classes are rare and the groups are quite task oriented. Research relating to teacher workshops strongly suggests that extended training experiences (one week or longer) with ample time for personal reflection are critical if change is to take place.

*Tips for Teacher Workshops*

- Provide the maximum possible access to the museum's resources, including yourself.

- Create a welcoming environment with comfortable seating, an array of teaching materials to peruse, and refreshments.

- Provide supplies and varied activities that are appropriate to the teacher's needs.

- When appropriate, model effective teaching practices using objects.

- Elicit teacher ideas for altering activities to meet teachers' needs.

- Share success stories and personal teaching experiences that were difficult.

- Link new content to classroom-based activities and national education standards.

- Add time into the schedule for periodic personal reflection.

- Small gestures to boost morale—like an educator's museum pass—greatly contribute to good will and return visits with schoolchildren.

## Workshops for the General Public

Workshops may seem similar to classes but they imply that participants will be busy with hands-on activities or will be engaged in some type of project. Workshops may be scheduled to take place a certain number of hours per week over several weeks, or they may take place over several consecutive days.

The Denver Art Museum offers a five-day photography workshop with professional photographers. The first four sessions include a one-hour introductory talk and two hours of fieldwork. The final session is an informal review of student photos.

With funding from the National Science Foundation, Seattle's Pacific Science Center developed a "Science Education Community Leadership Program" offering science education workshops to staff members of community-based organizations serving youth from demographic groups seldom represented in the study of science. The workshop consists of 112 hours of hands-on experience designed for people with little or no experience in science or teaching. Adults who have had this training become part of a network of informal science educators in community-based organizations throughout the Puget Sound area. The Pacific Science Center also provides take-home materials so the organizations can conduct science activities at their own centers.

*Tips for Workshops for the General Public*

- Actively engage the participants: the very label "workshop" connotes involvement.

- Use the richly varied backgrounds of participants and their potential power to accomplish goals.

- Avoid distractions; keep the group focused on the task at hand.

- Provide all participants with a list of where they can obtain the supplies to continue their projects at home.

- Make sure participants go home with a memento (e.g., a certificate or bookmark) from the museum to remind them of their time there.
- Use the museum Web site for follow-up materials.

## Performing Arts

Musical events, dance performances, and poetry readings can draw a variety of people to a museum. Offerings vary from a rock-and-roll band on the lawn to a chamber orchestra in an auditorium, or from a clog-dance demonstration to a major ballet company performance. Performing arts may or may not reflect a current exhibition, artifact, or theme of the museum. An art museum may use dance to interpret a work of art, an anthropology museum may include dance as part of an exhibit of a particular culture, or the ballet may be in town and need a large stage. Of the 116 museums whose staff we interviewed, slightly more than 65 percent offered performing arts programs for adults.

At the Joslyn Art Museum, the "Bagels & Bach" series presents a light brunch and a concert. This concert series, the only year-round opportunity in Omaha to hear live classical music, is open to museum members

Joe Gerling and Mike Pace, assistant chief–Delaware, who is dressed in clothing of a southern straight dancer. The Academy of Western Art is a series of adult artist workshops at the National Cowboy Hall of Fame and Western Heritage Museum, Oklahoma City. Four times a year, the center hosts a Western artist from the Museum's Prix de West show who uses museum classrooms to conduct an in-depth workshop while demonstrating his or her own skills. (Courtesy National Cowboy Hall of Fame and Western Heritage Museum.)

and nonmembers. The museum also offers a monthly jazz program and "First Friday JAMs." The Reynolda House Midnight Programs offer special performances for third-shift employees of hospitals, computer centers, and other companies that operate around the clock.

*Tips for Performing Arts Offerings*

- Study the museum's and community's needs and potential interests in such events.

- Cooperate with other community agencies in selecting and scheduling events.

- Develop a policy for the use of museum facilities by outside groups.

- When appropriate, make connections to other museum collections and programs.

Performances and concerts are especially effective program formats for evoking emotion and memories in adults. This reflective action is essential for adults to make sense of new ideas.

## Seminars and Symposia

Seminars and symposia derive from the idea that, when a group of informed people are brought together and stimulated to interact, good things happen. The two terms are often used interchangeably, though seminars are traditionally less formal. A seminar is a small group led by an informed discussion leader in which a particular concept, museum exhibit, or research idea is explored. Symposia are usually larger and more formal, typically consisting of series of short presentations by several persons on related topics or various phases of the same topic. Presentations are usually designed to stimulate discussion among attendees and may include lectures, panel discussions, classes, films, and demonstrations.

The success of seminars and symposia depend on the presenters' willingness to address varied aspects of the subject and participants' acceptance of diverse input. Time is usually allowed for interaction among presenters and participants. Slightly more than 63 percent of the museums in our survey offer symposia, while 54 percent offer seminars.

The Buffalo Bill Historical Center offers an annual weekend seminar on Plains Indian cultures. One particular seminar focused on the images drawn, painted, quilled, or beaded on tipis, clothing, tools, weapons, winter counts, and ledger books. The program included films, demonstrations, and lectures from at least seventeen different presenters. Program formats that introduce multiple perspectives can help adults become more critically reflective. Transformative learning is typically a social process that requires personal time to reflect on beliefs and meaning schemes.

### Tips for Seminars and Symposia

- The effectiveness as well as the appeal of a seminar or symposium is usually based on the interactions among speakers and other participants.

- Having a diversity of presenters enables the audience to gain a wide range of insights.

- Short presentations expressing varied insights keeps listeners alert and stimulated.

- The moderator or organizer must coordinate meticulously both time and content, to avoid repetitious presentations or schedule disruptions.

- Schedule frequent breaks with refreshments to encourage discussion.

- Introduce objects into seminar discussion to reinforce museum connections.

## Film Series

A film series usually consists of several films designed to enhance appreciation for a subject related to a museum exhibit or collection or based on a specific theme. Besides the more predictable lectures and discussions that often follow films, some museums offer appropriate food, drink, dance, or other participatory activities. Forty-six percent of the museums we interviewed offered film series.

The American Museum of Natural History sponsors the Margaret Mead Film and Video Festival. Screenings in 1998 were held at the museum and included films and videos from Poland, Haiti, Argentina, Taiwan, France, and other nations. Most sessions included discussions with the film directors.

The Denver Art Museum offered the Portraits of British Film series in conjunction with its exhibit "*600 Years of British Painting.*" All programs were introduced by a local newspaper film critic and concluded with a discussion.

*Tips for Film Series Programs*

- Provide a brief orientation to or outline of each film.

- Create relevant settings and activities to enhance the total effect of the films.

- Give participants an opportunity to ask questions and express their feelings about the films.

- Be aware that social and cultural issues affect both the mind and emotions.

Well-selected documentary, science, or art film has the power to take individuals on a personal journey and open them up to change. Discussion afterward helps adults integrate their related experiences and examine what is personally important.

### Classes

Both credit and noncredit classes are very popular types of museum adult programs and come in a variety of shapes, sizes, lengths, formats, and subjects. They are generally theme based, relating to a museum's exhibits, collections, or mission. Classes can provide adults with a closer look at objects, teach skills, offer recreation and social activity, and present an escape from daily concerns.

Credit classes are usually offered through the museum in conjunction with a local or regional university, college, or accrediting institution and are generally longer than one day. Forty-six percent of the 116 museums we interviewed offer credit classes.

The Buffalo Bill Historical Center offers two-week classes through the Larom Summer Institute in Western Studies in which students can earn

*Giant Steps Program, Yale University Art Museum.* (Courtesy Yale University Art Museum.)

undergraduate and graduate credit from the University of Wyoming or Montana State University. Classes have included "The Western Hero," "From Open Range to Feedlot: Western Cattle Ranching, 1850–1990," "Prehistoric Rock Art: Pictographs and Petroglyphs in the Intermountain West," and "Native American Tribalism: Emerging Paradigms of a New Indian Society in the 21st Century."

The Reynolda House offers American Foundations, an accredited graduate course in the summer session at Wake Forest University. This four-and-one-half-week program is limited to twenty students and focuses on history, literature, and music.

More commonly, museums sponsor noncredit classes. They offer a great variety of topics, and class length can range from one day upward. Fifty-eight percent of the museums we interviewed offer noncredit classes.

Two key elements of good museum classes are content organization and active engagement of course participants. Proper content organization takes into account the needs and interests of participants as well as the logical structuring of the subject matter. For each class, we highly recommend conducting a formal or informal assessment of learners' knowledge and personal learning objectives. This can be as simple as having participants introduce themselves and tell why they have joined the class. Insights into the levels and abilities of participants can also be gained by having participants perform a related task, or through a question-and-answer period.

*Tips for Improving Classes*

- Meet with the instructor in advance to review your educational goals and facility logistics (see appendix A for more details).

- Provide teaching materials and ready access to teaching collections.

- Encourage the instructor to vary teaching methods to include active participation, such as hands-on activities and small-group discussion.

- Personally welcome participants, distribute name tags, and spend some time interacting with the class along with the instructors.

- Invite participants to share their experiences, either through questions and answers, one-on-one critiques, evaluations, or storytelling.

- Create a physically and emotionally comfortable, nonthreatening learning environment and make sure your contract instructor supports this.

- Tell your instructor that you want to keep the class fun, challenging, and exciting.

Meaning perspectives are often the result of past education. Through classes, adults can experiment with new ideas, skills, and experiences that allow them to reconsider presuppositions.

## Beyond Bread-and-Butter: More Program Examples

In addition to the more traditional types of museum programs described above, project researchers participated in dozens of innovative and creative adult programs and many more were described to us. Some relied on collaboration with other agencies. Others focused specifically on promoting personal growth, fostering social interaction, or encouraging cultural enrichment. Others were dedicated to serving the mission of community service, while the main purpose of others was simply to have fun. We share some samples of these programs below with the hope that they may stimulate your own creative thinking.

### Collaborative Programs

Collaboration between museums and businesses, schools, community groups, government agencies, and other organizations often leads to innovative and successful programming. By sharing staff, resources, and clientele, collaborators can produce community-wide events that would otherwise be beyond reach. The cultural enrichment of the community, social interaction among diverse groups, and personal growth among individuals can create a momentum leading to further success.

Because of the increasing complexity of modern society, collaboration can greatly increase a program's effectiveness. In a *Museum News* article on challenges and strategies for the twenty-first century, the importance of collaboration was mentioned repeatedly. Ellsworth Brown, president of the Carnegie Museums of Pittsburgh, described the natural history museum of the twenty-first century as "collaborative, . . . accountable, . . . connected to issues of current and critical interest to humankind, . . . (and) activist."[1]

Ellen Futter, president of the American Museum of Natural History, supported this view by pointing to the important role of museums in the biodiversity crisis, claiming "collaboration of a diverse community has perhaps never been so necessary."[2] David Chesebrough, executive director of the Roberson Museum and Science Center, emphasized the word "partnerships." "When done properly," he remarks, "partnerships offer multiple benefits to a museum in achieving its mission, including attracting new audiences, improving connections with the community, and improving ways to fulfill a museum's mission, to the benefit of all."[3]

Programmers who recognize the museum's role as a community resource are more likely to initiate collaborative programs. There seems to be a connection between collaboration, concern for people and community, and innovation.

One of the broadest collaborative efforts we witnessed was conducted by the Field Museum of Natural History in Chicago. The Field Museum was hosting a traveling exhibit developed by the Holocaust Memorial called "*Assignment Rescue: The Story of Varian Fry and the Emergency Rescue Committee.*" Fry had been instrumental in helping artists, playwrights, and musicians escape from Nazi-occupied France. Working with cooperating institutions in the Chicago area, the Field Museum developed a series of programs including storytelling sessions, lectures, dialogues, panels, films, and field trips. The Art Institute of Chicago presented dramatic readings, lectures, and slides relating to the works of artists rescued by Varian Fry. Additional institutions sponsored programs related to "*Assignment Rescue,*" including the Block Museum of Art at Northwestern University, DePaul University, the Chicago Opera Theater, the Chicago Symphony Orchestra, the Film Center at the Art Institute of Chicago, the Marshall Jewish Learning Center, the Museum of Contemporary Art, the Smart Museum of Art, and the Spertus Institute of Jewish Studies.

The collaboration affected both individuals and the community. One participant was inspired to search out paintings, music, and plays produced by the artists who might have been lost without Fry. And leaders of the Field Museum's Center for Cultural Understanding and Change began to meet regularly with other cultural groups throughout the community.

In Tacoma, Washington, the "Consortium Partnership" linked the Washington State Historical Society, KCTS-Seattle Public TV, and the University of Washington Press for the purpose of producing products related to the centennial celebration of Mt. Rainier National Park. Working together, they created an exhibit with related educational programs, a documentary film, and a book.

*"Strike a Pose." This was part of a collaborative program between the Amon Carter Museum, Oakhurst Elementary, and the North Texas Institute for Educators on the Visual Arts (NTIEVA). The program was intended to allow mothers to take their children to see art for free in downtown Fort Worth. (Courtesy Amon Carter Museum.)*

The General Crook Museum in Nebraska reports that cooperative ventures with community clubs can raise the image of the club while attracting nonmuseum goers to the museum. For example, the Crazy Quilters, a local quilting group, staged an exhibition at the museum with their own quilts as well as quilts in the museum's collection. The quilters held demonstrations and were responsible for educating the public on the exhibit. According to the museum, both club and museum benefited. The museum acquired new members and additional funding while the clubs also drew new members. As many as four thousand people have attended such events. Collaborations can change the community's perception of the museum from impenetrable, exclusive institution to community resource.

Libraries and museums make natural partners. The "Writers on Site Program" is organized by the Oakland Museum of California in collaboration with the Oakland Public Library and privately owned Poets & Writers, Inc. The program uses poetry workshops and readings to explore self-expression in art and writing. Poets & Writers, Inc., covers all program costs so participants can attend free. Each year, three writers are chosen who, together with museum staff, decide on writing workshops, performances, symposia, and public readings.

Cooperative ventures need not be major events. "Sunday Strolls on Silver Strand State Beach" resulted from a cooperative arrangement between the Chula Vista Nature Center and Loews Coronado Bay Resort. Free nature walks are offered twice a week to hotel guests as well as people from the community. The program does not make money for the museum, but the interpretive guides (docents) receive a coupon for brunch or dinner for two at the hotel, worth about $70, each time they lead a walk. Docents enjoy the perk and the nature center gets good exposure. The success of the walks has inspired the hotel to offer additional programs and has inspired other docent groups in San Diego to try to establish similar programs with other hotels.

### Socially Interactive Programs

Our research confirmed that adult museum programs are social events for most participants. Even individuals attending lectures were most satisfied when there was time for discussion and interaction. In fact, program participants commented that more could sometimes be learned after the presentation than during the program itself. This supports the important concept that the exchange of ideas in socially supportive but challenging interactions is highly conducive to transformative learning. People seldom transform ideas in isolation. Educators Mihaly Csikszentmihalyi and Kim Hermanson see this as another important aspect of the meaning making, socializing role of museums: "Perhaps one of the major underdeveloped functions of museums is to provide opportunities for individually meaningful experiences that also connect with the experiences of others."[4]

Food and drink definitely add to the social nature of any gathering. More and more museums are offering their facilities as social gathering places by inviting adults in for food and drink. We observed one practice that could be widely integrated into existing programs: after a forty-five-minute presentation, attendees were invited to spend fifteen to twenty minutes mingling, conversing, and enjoying cookies and punch in the rear of the auditorium. The group reassembled after the break and a question period began. It was obvious that the movement, conversation, and refreshments made for a more enlivened discussion than had the discussion begun immediately after the presentation.

Every Wednesday night, the Oregon Museum of Art on the campus of the University of Oregon hosts "MusEvenings!" Snacks and drinks are offered along with the evening's program, which may be an art talk, musical program, lecture, relaxation class, poetry reading, dance, gallery talk, or other presentation. Participants have plenty of time for interaction over the course of the evening. The goals of "MusEvenings!" are to involve the campus community in museum activities and to promote increased use of museum collections by academic personnel. People not directly associated with the university are also welcomed to the museum through programs aimed at young couples or elders. On our visit we found one group of visitors viewing an exhibit of works by the university's master of fine arts students, while another group took part in a tai chi program. A retiree who was a regular visitor to MusEvenings! said his major reason for attending was to meet people with whom he could have intellectual discussions. Some of those discussions had induced him to subscribe to an art journal, even though art was not his primary interest.

The Birch Aquarium at Scripps Institution of Oceanography offers "Dive After Five" for guests twenty-one and older. This program gives adults some museum time free from the distracting crush of children and other visitors. Guests gather in an amphitheater in front of the kelp-forest tank and a docent or aquarist conveys questions to radio-equipped divers in the tank and reports their responses. The event is primarily social; the whole evening lasts two to three hours, although only about forty-five minutes are spent in front of the tank. Drinks and hors d'oeuvres are provided.

Some museums stimulate audience discussion on new ways of looking at art or a related topic. "Point of View Gallery Talks" at the J. Paul Getty Museum in Los Angeles are designed to provide an opportunity for the general public to experience works of art while interacting with artists and other nonmuseum professionals. These talks have been offered once a month on Friday evenings in conjunction with "Friday Nights at the Getty," which target a college-age audience. According to organizer Jill Finsten, "Although we have begun the program with visual artists (including a cinematographer), we intend to expand 'Points of View' to include writers, poets, musicians, and others who can provide a fresh perspective on the collection." These discussions are free to the public on a first-come first-served basis, but are offered a second time later in the evening.

### Personal and Cultural Development: Meaning Making and Transformation

In her book *From Knowledge to Narrative*, Lisa Roberts contends that the learning that occurs in museums often involves creating meaning for certain aspects of life rather than simply adding to knowledge. Such "meaning making" can help adults understand their place in the world.[5]

Several museum staffs we encountered purposefully incorporate opportunities for meaning making into their adult programs. They bring people
together for experiences with the specific objective of encouraging participants to reexamine and perhaps change their assumptions. Such presenters
tend to use multidisciplinary approaches to content and multimedia approaches in their delivery. In every case, special concern is given to ensuring
a supportive atmosphere.

The Baltimore Museum of Art and Sheppard Pratt Psychological Center cosponsor an innovative community service program that uses gallery
walks and art workshops to help people understand their eating disorders. A
museum docent and Sheppard Pratt staff member usually plan the workshops together. Participants typically view specific works of art in the galleries and then express themselves through clay regarding the art and their
eating disorders.

The staff of the Reynolda House Museum of American Art uses contemporary American art to get people to examine societal prejudice. In a
program titled "Examining Prejudice through Looking at American Art,"
participants first take a solo journey through the museum's collections,
recording their feelings about the art on a form provided. Participants
then come together in small groups to share their reactions. It is a revela-
tion to many participants that others relate differently, not only to the art
itself but also to the art's messages. Participants then work together to
study one particular painting, selected by the group. From resources supplied by the museum, they gather information about the artist as well as
the music, literature, and history of the time. This leads to a discussion of
possible racial, gender, age, religious, or class prejudices reflected in the
work. The small groups then present their findings to the whole group
while a slide of the painting is projected on a screen. Reynolda House staff
may invite representatives of different ethnic or cultural minorities to
share with the group their experiences with prejudice.

Participants in the "Examining Prejudice" program are encouraged to
respond with their own stories or questions or to write in a journal about
the experience. Refreshments are provided and the program is conducted
in a comfortable, attractive setting. This program has drawn over two
thousand participants since 1985 and has become a model for programs
examining reactions to art and culture.

The "Community Forum Program" at the Andy Warhol Museum engages mostly local participants from various backgrounds, including writers,

artists, and other professionals, in discussions about art, culture, and contemporary issues. For example, a discussion on cloning featured an artist, a priest, and a biologist. Regularly scheduled for the first Thursday of every month, Community Forums provide a rich environment in which personal transformation and meaning making can occur. The museum also views this program as a successful and effective outreach vehicle that builds community awareness.

The programs mentioned above have specific goals of transformative learning and seem to promote the objectives stated in *Excellence and Equity*. This 1992 publication of the American Association of Museums demands

> a new definition of museums as institutions of public service and education, a term that includes exploration, study, observation, critical thinking, contemplation, and dialogue. Museums perform their most fruitful public service by providing an educational experience in the broadest sense: by fostering the ability to live productively in a pluralistic society and to contribute to the resolution of the challenges we face as global citizens. The public educational responsibility of the museum has two facets: excellence and equity. In every aspect of their operations and programs, museums must combine a tradition of intellectual rigor with the inclusion of a broader spectrum of our diverse society.[6]

But offering programs that focus on community issues could also be an occasion for museum professionals to consider why there is so little diversity in the adult audience attracted to museum programs. (See age and education levels of program participants in chapter 3.)

## Community Service and Outreach Programs

Generally, outreach is defined as any effort to take the museum's mission outside the walls of the institution. Lawrence Fang, associate director of the Oregon Museum of Art, defines outreach as (1) making programs available to members of the community not able to visit the museum, (2) soliciting community input into the museum's decision-making processes, and (3) inviting all community members to attend museum programs. Seventy-three percent of the museums included in our survey offered some type of outreach program for adults.

Outreach programs may be offered in nursing homes, hospitals, businesses, clubs, and other facilities. Museums might provide traveling exhibits and teaching trunks and loan museum resources or collections. The Museum

of New Mexico, for example, has a forty-foot van that travels to rural communities throughout New Mexico. The van stays in one community for several days at a time to help local community members develop local exhibits
based on objects, experiences, history, and personal memories. Midnight
Programs at the Reynolda House offer special performances for third-shift
employees of hospitals, computer centers, and other twenty-four-hour enterprises.

Most museums view themselves as community organizations with
community service missions. Partnerships between communities and museums have existed since the earliest days of American museums and are
becoming even more important today. David Chesebrough writes, "Museums, as publicly supported institutions, have been urged to play a larger
role in solving community problems, particularly in the essential areas of
education and economic development."[7] To put such a mission into action
demands more than a few simple links with convenient local groups. Museums need to give serious thought to the needs of their various "communities." Claudine Brown offered a definition of "community" some years
ago, explaining that community can be made up of individuals who share
a common history or common societal, economic, or political interests.
Brown writes that community is not solely an ethnic group, a neighborhood, or the residents of a defined area. As she puts it, from the moment
we are born we are involved with one community or another and with
many different communities at once.[8]

Today's complex society is made up of an incredibly diverse array of communities with vastly different needs. The Philadelphia Museum of Art offers
monthly workshops for elderly adults, people with mental or developmental
disabilities, and people living with AIDS. Programs may involve a tour,
hands-on studio experience, movement, interactive theatre, or creative writing. The Form in Art program provides studio and gallery classes for blind
and visually impaired adults.

The J. Paul Getty Museum has developed a program called Community Collaboration Workshops. Designed for leaders of community-based
organizations, the workshops demonstrate ways in which community
groups can utilize the museum's collections and educational services.
Workshop attendees participate in gallery lessons, practice designing a
museum lesson tailored for their constituency, learn about the logistics of
leading their group on a tour, and receive materials including handbooks,
posters, and gallery lessons. Organizations can send up to four people to a

workshop. Attendees are eligible to receive funding for one bus to the museum with their constituents. These four-hour, Saturday workshops are offered quarterly.

In the "Horticultural Therapy Program," the Tucson Botanical Gardens offers sessions on herbs, houseplants, succulents, and holiday craft activities in nursing homes and hospitals, and also reaches participants through the Arthritis Foundation. One staff person supervises twenty docents who conduct the programs in different facilities throughout Tucson. Taking programs outside museum walls like this can build public perception of the museum as a community partner. For the docent, community building often leads to personal growth and makes them more effective contributors to society.

*Tips for Outreach Programs*

- Maintain the same high standards for outreach programs as are set for programs within the museum.

- Know the audience. Because the outreach audience may differ from the typical in-house museum audience, audience studies may be necessary.

- Study the museum's area of service to identify audiences with needs for outreach services.

- Design special outreach programs for underserved groups or communities in the vicinity of the museum.

### Programs for Adults with Special Needs

Special-needs adults want to learn and are able to learn. Program planners can be sensitive to special needs while still offering challenging and stimulating experiences that can lead to transformation and meaning making. Special-needs programs need not be watered down.

The Los Angeles County Museum of Art offers a comprehensive "Art for All" program for people with visual impairments, hearing impairments, mental disabilities, physical disabilities, and learning disabilities. "Art for All" offers gallery tours, slide-illustrated lectures, and art workshops focused on special exhibitions or on aspects of the museum's permanent collection. All programs are free of charge, although reservations are required. Tours last about one hour and are structured to encourage visitor participation. Depending on participants' needs, tour guides use a variety of interactive techniques, including questioning strategies, hands-on objects, and dialoguing. Gallery tours incorporating tactile experiences and spoken interpretation are offered for the visually impaired. Tours with sign-language interpreters are available on request.

## Theater Programs

*Dramatic Presentations*

Dramatic presentations are becoming more popular in museum education and may include museum theater, living-history performances,

*Dancers from the Dallas Black Dance Theatre perform* Mary, Don't You Weep *at a symposium at the Dallas Museum of Art. This event was part of a two-week city festival called* Art and Soul 2000 *that brought the diverse peoples of Dallas together for song, dance, lectures, symposia, and exhibitions to explore the common yearning for a relationship with the divine. (Courtesy Dallas Museum of Art.)*

plays, or storytelling. These types of programs are effective with large groups of adults and are a good way to present difficult subject matter in a nonthreatening manner. Performances might relate to a current exhibit, artifact, or theme and can take place anywhere within the museum, in an exhibit, lobby, or theater or on the lawn. Slightly more than 50 percent of the museums we investigated were using dramatic presentations.

Dramatic performances tend to have a long-lasting learning effect on audiences because of their emotional impact. Colonial Williamsburg's living-history program, "Enslaving Virginia," depicts costumed characters as slave owners and slave leaders while admission-paying tourists play the role of slaves. This program has evoked such strong emotions that some audience members have attacked actors playing the role of slave owners.

More and more educators are finding that drama adds "flow" to the museum experience. University of Chicago psychology professor Mihaly Csikszentmihalyi's concept of a "flow experience" involves becoming caught up and totally engaged in a challenging yet pleasing experience. Such intense physical, emotional, and intellectual attentiveness can dramatically enhance learning.

## Bringing Stories to Life

We had been to this museum only once before, but a new exhibit on the "Negro in Baseball" attracted us back. It was fascinating to learn how a Negro baseball league was formed in 1932 and that no black players entered the majors until 1947, when Jackie Robinson went to bat for the Brooklyn Dodgers. We've seen exhibits before, but what made this one special was a live theater performance by an actor playing Satchel Paige, the first black inducted into the National Baseball Hall of Fame.

"Satchel" recalled the days of old, told us of the many hardships endured by the men who played the game, and whose access to the major leagues had been denied for so long. His performance was brilliant and his anecdotes funny. His perspective caused us to think about things we wouldn't have without seeing such life experiences through his eyes. One of the most interesting aspects was interacting with "Satchel," as we had the opportunity to ask him questions. The exhibit and ideas presented in the exhibit became meaningful to us through this actor's dramatization.

Catherine Hughes of the Museum of Science, Boston, wholeheartedly supports the use of theater in museums:

> Theatre is alive, relevant, and familiar, all qualities for which museums today aspire. . . . Its power is to allow us to view human interactions and make judgments about situations we may or may not have experienced, but that we can relate to and into which we can easily imagine ourselves. It touches on the collective human experience.[9]

Theater presentations can be excellent vehicles for personal transformation. Human beings commonly create meaning in their lives through metaphor or analogy rather than through syllogism (deductive reasoning) or formal argument. Storytelling can help people reflect on the roots of their own assumptions.

---

## CASE STUDY 2.2

### "Mapping the Soul," a Play by Jon Lipsky, Presented at the Science Museum of Minnesota

#### General Description

"Mapping the Soul" is a twenty-minute, one-act play exploring the pros and cons of science, particularly the Human Genome Project. The play begins in a young couple's home with the husband getting ready for work. As he is about to leave, the wife asks him to quit his job with the Human Genome Project. The actors then explain the project, along with its potential benefits and societal problems. No conclusions are drawn as to what is right or wrong; rather the play exposes the audience to a broad perspective on science. Participation and introspection are encouraged, as twice during the performance the actors solicit audience comment and opinion. Given in an auditorium adjacent to a museum exhibit hall, the performance is included with museum admission.

#### Institutional Perspective

Science theater and emotion have a definite place in the museum, but emotion must take a secondary role in science education and can't be gratuitous. Ideal programs are relevant, enjoyable, valuable, and memorable.

*continued*

## Production Director's Perspective

The mission of the museum is to educate people about science. We offer a twist that adds something unexpected to the learning experience. We want to present the humanity behind the science and bring an emotional quality to the museum that has been absent. The big challenge is balancing facts and entertainment.

In presenting programs that examine public policy issues like the Human Genome Project or fetal tissue research, we try to present all sides. We ask dangerous, provocative questions in order to make people think. In the exhibit hall we celebrate science, in the theater we question it.

## Participants' Perspectives

I. Joe
Age: twenty-nine
Education: college graduate
Occupation: student

The show made me think twice about my views on the Human Genome Project and science in general. It opened my eyes about the controversy surrounding the project and made me change my way of thinking about scientific progress. The acting was excellent. It was one of the best theatrical experiences I've ever had and was definitely the most moving experience I've had in a science museum.

2. Jane
Age: thirty-five
Education: postgraduate degree
Occupation: teacher

The play was provocative in its approach and was able to display different views on the controversial subject of genetic engineering and the Human Genome Project. The acting was excellent, but I was disappointed that the play was so short. It left me hanging; I wanted more factual information about genetic technology and the Human Genome Project.

## Research Observation

The emotional response from the audience was very powerful. At times, the play was psychologically uncomfortable because of the combination of presentation, introspection, and discussion. During the two "breaks" when

*continued*

CASE STUDY 2.2 (continued)

actors solicited opinions and comments from the audience, the actors became guides and facilitators.

One of the actors was more convincing than the other, making the play as a whole seem somewhat biased. In an interview, the director explained that the less-convincing actor was new and not as comfortable in the improvisational aspects of the show, and that no bias was intended.

**Analysis**

"Mapping the Soul" offered a counterpoint to the typical "science is fascinating and wonderful" outlook of science museums. Museum theater programs bridge the gap between experiential and didactic learning by presenting facts while fostering introspection and self learning. Drama and emotion can be powerful tools in educating audiences, but the trick is in effectively blending together facts, emotions, plot, topic, and acting. It is interesting that the institutional perspective indicated a desire to be careful about allowing too much emotion into the museum, while the director of the play saw emotion as the most powerful tool available to science theater.

The quality of the acting is critical in any theater presentation and museum science theater is no exception. Our research observer felt that while the acting was exceptional, the play was slightly biased toward the viewpoint offered by the stronger actor. This would be a danger in all theater programs attempting to present balanced views.

---

The Science Museum of Minnesota has a long history of using theater and drama to interpret both the museum's exhibits and the institution's purpose. A staff of five full-time theater professionals use drama in daily presentations to children and adults. The museum holds an annual seminar for other educators who wish to develop theater programs of their own. When asked what she hopes happens in dramatic presentations at the museum, Director of Public Programs Tessa Bridal replies, "Make people enthusiastic!"

*"Guerilla" Theater*

Infusing museum programs with "theater" doesn't have to involve staging a play. Expressive gestures and the dramatic use of voice and props can grab and hold an audience's attention in any situation. With a touch of drama, a young woman we observed brought an incredible degree of life and meaning to a Hmong exhibit at the Science Museum of Minnesota. She told the story of "her father," an American pilot who crashed in the mountains and was rescued by Hmong villagers, who hid him, nursed him back to health, and later led him back to safe territory across American lines. So mesmerizing and convincing was her delivery that our researcher didn't realize until days later that she was not really the pilot's daughter.

The Andy Warhol Museum in Pittsburgh has pushed the idea of performance and interaction within a gallery with its "15 Minutes Plus" program, which provides artists of various disciplines an opportunity to present their work in a museum gallery. Each artist is encouraged to perform—as a dancer, artist, filmmaker, musician, poet, or whatever—in the context of an exhibit. The Museum staff believes such presentations by varied artists can evoke a spirit of creative license. Dramatic presentations do require a great deal of preparation and planning. Programs are usually developed in-house, but some museums may collaborate with a local theater group.

*Tips for Successful Dramatic Performances*

- Actively involve museum visitors through role-playing, question and answer, or discussion.

- Use trained actors if possible.

- Conduct performances in a way that shows concern for the audience's emotions and understanding of the subject matter.

- Use eye-catching scenery, props, and costumes.

- Have someone really talented write the play.

## Elderhostel Programs

Our study showed that people over sixty-five years of age are a significant segment of museum audiences. Programs for seniors, especially extensive Elderhostel and travel programs, allow museums to serve this important audience while sending the message that age is no barrier to learning.

Elderhostel is a nonprofit organization committed to providing high-quality, affordable, educational opportunities to older adults. Each quarterly Elderhostel catalog invites seniors to participate in any of approximately two dozen programs that it coordinates with museums. For example, Boston's Museum of Science hosted a triple Elderhostel program involving a look behind the scenes, an exploration of a special exhibit, and demonstrations on the properties of water. The Pink Palace Museum in Memphis invited Elderhostel participants to be "curator for a week," in their program, "Curator for a

*Elderhostel—Meriwether Lewis in Blackfeet Country. A day at Camp Disappointment ends each year with a ranch-style barbecue and entertainment by Jack Gladstone at the Two Medicine River.* (Courtesy Glacier County Historical Museum.)

Week: Behind the Scenes at a Natural History and History Museum." (Many people are interested in what goes on behind the scenes in a museum.)

At the Stuhr Museum of the Prairie Pioneer in Grand Island, Nebraska, one weeklong Elderhostel program included packing a handcart, cooking in a Dutch oven, and taking a bus to nearby sites along the Oregon Trail. Toward the end of the week, participants got the contrasting view by touring modern, computerized farms and feedlots to understand how agriculture is managed in this century.

Boston's Museum of Science began its involvement with older audiences gradually by collaborating with retirement communities that bused people in for special programs. Now it hosts several Elderhostels a year and appreciates the fact that Elderhostel handles all the logistics.

The Museum of Science and Industry (MOSI), Tampa, uses a different approach to Elderhostels. Instead of holding their own, they collaborate with other agencies offering the programs. Many Elderhostel programs study two or three topics each session, so MOSI might invite participants into the museum two or three times during a weeklong program.

### Exhibitions and Programs for Older Adults

Some suggestions for developing exhibitions and programs for older adults from Gretchen Jennings, project director at the Smithsonian Institution's Lemelson Center for the Study of Invention and Innovation:

- Recognize diversity, with widely varying individual differences. The category of people classified as "older" spans decades. People in their nineties, no matter how fit, will probably have greater special needs than those in their sixties.
- Separate the concept of "ailing" from that of "aging" and know the specific audience of older adults you are targeting. A program tailored to frail and confused residents in a retirement home will not be appropriate for the healthy and active adults who may live there as well.
- Recognize the tremendous interest that many older adults have in continuing to learn and tap into that for purposes of audience development, volunteer recruitment, and employment.
- Including senior advisers on exhibition and program development teams can help insure that resources targeted to older audiences are not ageist or patronizing.
- For a variety of reasons, higher education levels continue to be correlated with healthy aging and longevity. For museums, which tend to attract a highly educated public, this is another indicator that older audiences will only increase in the coming years. It is also a reminder that programs for underserved audiences should not be limited to the young.

## Festivals and Special Events

The core purpose of many museums is to acknowledge and celebrate the people, history, and accomplishments of the area. As a sign in one museum put it, "Here is who we were. Here is who we are. Ain't it great!" Even museums with other central missions can strengthen their ties to the community by sponsoring or participating in community events.

Festivals and special events can serve large groups of adults, although they are generally open to all ages. They are usually theme oriented (Earth Day, Native American, Latin American) and relate more to the museum's mission than to any particular exhibit. These types of programs are a great way to learn about different cultures and provide multisensory experiences because they often involve food, music, arts and crafts, and games. In addition, festivals can be great collaborative events with community partners. Festivals and special events can be one-day events or longer. When the town of Alexandria, Virginia, celebrated its 250th anniversary, local museums organized programs on that theme throughout the year.

The Smithsonian Institution has put on its annual, two-week Folklife Festival since 1980. This program is generally family oriented and focuses on one state and two different countries each year. Festival events include games, arts and crafts, storytelling, music, food, and interpretive signs.

The University of Wyoming Geological Museum and Art Museum and the Western Heritage Center have collaborated on such events as a Fall Fest and Haunted Prison in October, a Holiday Wine Fest and Olde-Fashioned Family Christmas in November, and Christmas Dinner Theatre in December. At a July "Vintage Baseball Game," everyone including the umpire and a woman calling the team members to bat wore baseball costumes from the turn of the century. Audience members were provided with a list of turn-of-the century terms for baseball players and plays and participated by cheering the teams.

Each fall, the Museum of the Rockies invites the community to gather at their living-history farm to celebrate life in early Montana. Reenactors demonstrate wheat harvesting, blacksmithing, and animal care. In the restored, hewn-log Tinsley House, people sample food cooked on the woodstove and play old-fashioned family games. Gardeners study the carefully planned and planted heritage garden.

Along with historically or seasonally themed events, cultural celebrations also offer occasions for community get-togethers. The Eiteljorg Museum of American Indians and Western Art in Indianapolis celebrates the food, customs, and practices of different groups through events such as "authentic Native American harvest meals." This includes a forty-five-minute cooking demonstration, with samples for observers. Buffet meals follow for an extra fee.

*Las Posadas*, a Christmas tradition among some Spanish-speaking groups, has been cohosted by the Eiteljorg Museum and St. Patrick Church. In *Las Posadas*, participants recreate in song the story of Joseph and Mary searching Bethlehem for a place to stay. A procession of singers walks along a designated route in Indianapolis, stopping at door after door to ask if there is room at the inn. A singing denial comes from the other side of each door, until the last doorway, which opens in welcome. That door has been the Eiteljorg Museum. Inside the museum, young people take turns swinging at a candy-filled piñata and the museum store is open for holiday shopping.

In community celebrations, a spectrum of people shares experiences, reminisces about the past, and speculates on the future. Celebrations can introduce the museum to a broader audience and foster a feeling among community members that the museum is relevant to their lives.

*Tips for a Good Festival*

- Include a wide range of community members in the planning and development of community festival events.

- Schedule the event to be sensitive to related social and cultural issues.

- Consider providing an early-bird program for seniors.

- Good public relations and publicity are crucial for successful events.

- If the festival is really a family event, it is important to have interactive, hands-on activities for all ages.

## Field Schools

Field schools provide a unique format for adult museum programming. However, only 11.5 percent of the museums we interviewed offered in-depth field experiences. Field schools are most often conducted by natural history and science and technology museums and are typically family oriented.

In a field school, participants live and work at a research site with anthropologists, paleontologists, and other professionals. This provides a great opportunity for hands-on experiences and close-quarters interaction with experts and other people with similar interests. Field schools generally last at least twenty-four hours and may be as long as several weeks. Program costs typically include housing and meals.

The Oregon Museum of Science and Industry offers a wide variety of field schools, covering topics from the exploration of Puget Sound to fossils and habitats of central Oregon. Program fees include instruction, field-study equipment, accommodations, admissions, and food.

Other exciting field-based programs are built around the idea of "citizen-science," in which participants contribute to real investigations while building knowledge and interest in their surroundings. Whether it is an urban park biodiversity study, a volunteer water-quality study in a city lake, a pigeon survey, or an insect survey, adults are attracted to well-organized experiences that allow them to use their time in meaningful and productive ways that are beneficial to the community.

Field schools are most effective as learning experiences when leaders share not only their expertise but also their subject-related problems and concerns. Building a compatible social and interactive atmosphere makes the experience very conducive to transforming participants' perspectives.

### Travel and Adventure Programs

Many adults today want their learning experiences to literally take them away. For this, they turn to such established organizations as Elderhostel, alumni associations, and museums. Museums can attract participants to travel or adventure programs by tying travel experiences to exhibits and offering ex-

Participants in the Museum of the Rockies' Paleo Field Program. (Courtesy Museum of the Rockies.)

pert guides (especially curators and educators) whom local people know and trust. Museums can also provide participants the opportunity to follow up on insights gained through their travel experience. We found that travel programs are not just nice vacations for affluent museum patrons, but also are often occasions of intensive learning and cathartic personal change. Just over 50 percent of the museums in our survey offered some sort of travel program for adults.

The goals of travel and adventure programs are generally to educate adults about the natural world, to enable them to experience new places, and to promote socially rewarding adventures. Travel programs generally last at least one week and may venture anywhere in the world. Some museums, like the San Diego Museum of Natural History, have carefully considered their core values for adult travel. As their tourist brochure emphasizes, "Our commitment is to travel lightly and leave a positive impact by spending locally for food, lodging, and remembrances, using local guides and outfitters whenever possible, and supporting citizen's organizations and governmental agencies with stewardship responsibilities through membership, service projects, education and research projects."[10]

Adult educators at the Science Museum of Minnesota view travel programs as excellent learning situations because they are fun, they involve activity, and the participants interact and learn about one another while they also learn about a topic. When the museum sponsored a tour to Aruba to witness a solar eclipse, two hundred people from seventeen states participated. Excitement about the trip led to a lot of learning beforehand:

> A real learning community came together for the week leading up to the solar eclipse. We springboarded from the eclipse event to natural history and the island of Aruba to cultural history. Some members of our group went out to the local schools to lecture and work with kids and teachers.

Travel programs require much planning, but when done well, they offer many opportunities for learning and may also positively affect the sites visited. Tours and travel programs frequently lead to collaborations on environmental and conservation issues between museums and community agencies. In a trip to La Mision, Mexico, a group from the San Diego Museum of Natural History studied plants and birds south of Tijuana, an area well-known for its estuary and biologically rich habitats. Guided by a museum scientist, they gathered data that would help the community prepare their request to gain federal reserve status for the area. The museum also reminds members that ecotourism begins at home and issues an open invitation to participate in regularly scheduled local nature walks and environmental events.

Historical events can also be an occasion for organizing travel programs. The bicentennial of the Lewis and Clark expedition is raising attention throughout the country, especially in areas where the Corps of Discovery actually traveled. The Museum of the Rockies organized a bus trip following the path of Lewis and Clark down the Missouri River from Fort Union in the northeast corner of Montana to the headwaters of the Missouri, near the southeast part of the state. Two leaders well versed in the past and present of the area contributed to the success of the trip, as did a very comfortable tour bus and stops at national and state historic sites and monuments. Participants took their meals together, adding to the sociability of the trip and giving people a relaxed opportunity to share insights and observations.

*Tips for Travel Programs*

- Carefully investigate the trustworthiness and reliability of travel agencies and tour guides.

- Begin informational and educational efforts as early as feasible. Participants should have at least one pretrip meeting to get information on the destinations, local history, necessary equipment, clothing, and cultural considerations.

- Build a spirit of cooperation and mutual assistance among all participants.

- Use restricted time (for example, travel time) for group building or education. However, allow for private time at various points in the day.

- Trip leaders should be familiar with sites ahead of time and be sensitive to issues of cultural difference.

### Virtual Travel Programs

Museums have discovered that you don't have to hit the road to put on a trip. "Travel programs" can be successful without leaving the building. To better display a special traveling exhibit on Claude Monet, the Minneapolis Institute of Art conducted a simulated tour of four areas that influenced Monet's art. In four different one-hour presentations, participants "traveled" to northwestern France, areas north of France (London and Norway), the Mediterranean, and Paris. Following each lecture, a reception was held in the museum's Fountain Court featuring the sounds and flavors of Monet's adventures, including period music and regional delicacies and hors d'oeuvres.

Similar programs may be offered by presenters well versed in the arts, music, and history of a region. Such "visits" can be made not only to different places, but to different periods of history.

## Certificate Programs

Certificate programs typically offer a selection of classes that result in their own certificate or count toward a certificate granted by various professional organizations. The New York Botanical Garden's Certificate Program is recognized by the New Jersey Board of Architects, the Association of Professional Landscape Design, the New York Recreational Therapy Association, the International Society of Arboriculture, and the New York and New Jersey Pesticide Recertification Agencies. For the purpose of this book, we have separated certificate programs from teacher workshops because the former are open to a variety of professionals.

In Chicago, about forty different organizations and institutions cooperate in sponsoring one certificate program. Participants can take a variety of ecology, botany, zoology, geology, and interpretation courses at the Field Museum, the Morton Arboretum, the Nature Conservancy, and other facilities. The program was originally designed by the local arboretum to train volunteers. Students must complete thirteen to fifteen courses in order to obtain a certificate.

## Book Signings, Discussions, Readings

Many museums offer book signings, discussions, and readings as a different approach to drawing adult audiences. Book discussions may be led by local professors or nationally known authors and may or may not be related to a museum exhibit or collection. Book readings and signings allow participants to hear nationally known or local authors and poets as they read from their work. In one example, the Field Museum offered a lecture and a signing of the book *Looking for Olmsted*, in conjunction with the temporary exhibit of the same title, on Frederick Law Olmsted.

## Seeds of Change

Wherever the idea comes from and whatever the topic, the seeds of program excellence are in the details. It's important to note that programs that bring adults together for several days at a time are more likely to produce significant change in people. This is especially true when participants are confined to a limited space and share everything from activities to meals.

Program formats are just one of the variables program planners consider in developing and implementing excellent museum programs. In chapter 3, we look at the program planner's roles and responsibilities.

## Notes

1. Ellsworth Brown, "Catalogue of Change," *Museum News* 76, no. 6 (1997): 36.

2. Ellen Futter, "Biodiversity," *Museum News* 76, no. 6 (1997): 41.

3. David Chesebrough, "Museum Partnerships: Insights from the Literature and Research," *Museum News* 77, no. 6. (1997): 53.

4. Mihaly Csikszentmihalyi and Kim Hermanson, "Intrinsic Motivation in Museums: What Makes Visitors Want to Learn?" *Museum News* 74, no. 3 (1995): 35.

5. Lisa C. Roberts, *From Knowledge to Narrative: Educators and the Changing Museum* (Washington, D.C.: Smithsonian Institution Press, 1997).

6. American Association of Museums, ed., *Excellence and Equity: Education and the Public Dimension of Museums* (Washington, D.C.: American Association of Museums, 1992).

7. Chesebrough, "Museum Partnerships," 51.

8. Brown, "Catalogue of Change," 36.

9. Catherine Hughes, *Museum Theatre* (Portsmouth, N.H.: Heinemann, 1998), 32.

10. San Diego Museum of Natural History, "Travel Brochure."

# CHAPTER THREE

# PROGRAM PLANNERS

> Program planners are very much like orchestra conductors. They must be able to bring together diverse players and pieces in a harmonious and balanced effort.
>
> —Rosemary Caffarella, adult education researcher

Today's program planners are often called on to be equal parts juggler, clairvoyant, educator, manager, salesperson, facilitator, and miracle worker. They must anticipate what the public wants and what the institution will agree to and create, develop, and produce a program, which they must then sell to an audience. In this chapter, program planners share their motivations, goals, and strategies. They outline their views on instructors and instructor support and reveal potential obstacles to developing and implementing successful programs. Nobody ever said it would be easy. (Guidelines for developing the programs themselves are presented in chapter 6.)

## Anatomy of a Program Planner: Who They Are and Why They Do What They Do

The majority of program planners surveyed were experienced, professional women. Twenty-five percent of respondents had been planning programs for five to ten years, 15 percent had eleven to fifteen years of experience, another 15 percent had sixteen to twenty years of experience, and 17 percent had been planning programs for twenty-one years or more. Most of these professionals had worked in a variety of formal and informal education settings.

Program planners also had high levels of education, but little formal training specifically in adult education. Nearly 50 percent had master's degrees and 9 percent held doctorates. These exceptionally high education levels are similar to those of program participants (see chapter 5), suggesting that program planners offer classes that cater to individuals similar to themselves. This finding is similar to others in adult education literature that most program planners rely on past experiences to create new program ideas. While this appears to be a common practice in museums, increased attention has been placed in recent years on audience surveys and evaluations. Audience studies have provided more information and direction for generating new programs. The most common assessment procedure is to offer programs and see how many and what types of adults enroll.

While a few of the larger museums have created staff positions for adult educators to develop adult-driven programs, most museum educators do myriad projects for youth and have little time for adult programs. Their typically taxing workloads leave little room for long-term program planning, evaluation, or remediation. As a result, only a handful of the planners we surveyed had written vision or mission statements for their programs. Written guidelines for instructors, use of teaching collections, and program evaluations were seldom found.

It was also uncommon to find program managers keeping written records or profiles on frequent adult program participants. While most program planners clearly know an enormous amount about their clients, because of time restraints this information is rarely recorded. With frequent staff turnover, the profiles of these individuals are lost.

Researchers also found a pervasive sense that education is still a second-tier program in museums. Time and again, organization policies created situations in which educators had fewer privileges. Frequently, they were paid less than were other staff, they had less funding for travel or professional development, and their job descriptions did not include research opportunities. Museum teaching spaces were often relegated to windowless basements, while board and administrative support was lacking. These common problems were not limited to any type or size of institution.

The primary reasons program planners gave for offering adult programs were educating the public, fostering community involvement, and facilitating learning and enjoyment. Some planners felt a responsibility to certain, select target groups, while others want to serve a broader audience. As one curator of education explained, programs are a way for the museum to build a solid base of community support and bring more diverse audiences together. For her, offering programs was a way for the museum to be a catalyst for the

*The educational mission is a major part of our long-range plan. All aspects of the museum's services are designed with an educational focus that considers all types of audiences, regardless of age, sex, physical barriers, race, or religious affiliation.*

Darla Bruner, education curator,
Historical Museum at Fort Missoula

community. Another planner envisioned the museum as a "university of the people," with planetarium programs centered around current events and the facility used as a resource for education and research. Said another planner, "You can show your community that you care about them and want to serve them through your programs."

Some program managers expressed their dedication to lifelong learning in terms of improved teaching. According to the director of education in one science museum, "We encourage instructors to adopt a new way of teaching with more hands-on experiments, more thinking about the experiments, and more interviewing of learners for years after."

A large number of planners viewed programs as a conduit to collections. One education director stated, "Adults develop more of an attachment to the museum if they have access to collections. The real stuff makes connections." An education specialist at a large art museum said, "Adult educational programs are a way of connecting the audience to our collections. We provide information and a bridge to those looking for information."

Many planners are truly dedicated to art, science, or history and hope to share this appreciation through their programming. The director of an art museum told us that she encourages programming that helps people engage their own creativity through forums or performances. Culture, she noted, finds its depths through the arts.

Along with the serious missions of education and transformation, most program planners also want mature learners to have fun while they learn and increase their awareness of their own lives and the world around them.

## Ten Steps toward Excellence

In general, museum program planners agree it's important to offer a variety of quality learning experiences that, ideally, transform participants into active, engaged learners. However, the type of programs that should be offered, the level of learning or transformation to strive for, and what segments of the community should be reached are continuing topics of discussion. No matter what approaches, levels, or strategies the planner settles on, the following guidelines can help bring the task into focus.

1. Define your mission, vision, and core values. Write them down. Articulate them daily to staff, funders, and adult program participants.

2. Train your contract staff so they can articulate your core values, mission, and vision.

3. Make sure instructors have access to teaching collections, exhibits, and key places behind the scenes.

4. Find out what the adults in your community care about and want to know more about.

5. Develop collaborative programs with community members to serve the four main types of adult museum program participants: knowledge seekers, socializers, skill builders, and museum lovers (see chapter 1).

6. Be a super host. Invest in comfortable furniture and provide refreshments. If possible, create teaching spaces in sunlit places.

7. Continually experiment with new programs, while building your list of annual places.

8. Broaden your circle of program advisers. Collaborate with new community groups frequently.

9. Check to see how much impact your programs are having by interviewing program participants six to eight weeks after the experience. Create and maintain participant profiles for repeat class consumers.

10. Strive to create the conditions under which life-changing experiences can take place.

## Organ Crawl, Science Museum of Minnesota

### General Description

The Organ Crawl provided an opportunity for participants to see, hear, and experience firsthand the history, repertoire, and construction of the pipe organ. In five separate tours, participants could view a total of twenty-six organs. Tours were designed to illustrate how different church congregations, buildings, and organ builders influenced individual instruments. The tours were held on Saturday afternoons and took about four-and-one-half hours each. Buses shuttled people from building to building where knowledgeable people conducted demonstrations. Fees for one tour were $16 for members, $20 for nonmembers. The cost for three tours was $46 for members and $55 for nonmembers. For a package of all five tours, cost was $75 for members and $90 for nonmembers.

### Institutional Perspective

The best programs involve activity in which all can be personally involved, preferably without sharing equipment. Socializing is very important and so is having fun.

Instructors have to know their content and be enthusiastic about it. They should take advantage of the adults' experience and be respectful of participants' experiences and perspectives. A good teacher loves the subject matter and makes it exciting for adults.

The biggest barriers to developing a successful museum adult education program are money and promotion. Often, not much effort goes into selling programs, but you have to spend money to make money. I frequently attend society and organization meetings to promote our programs. I'm a nuts-and-bolts person. I want programs to run in the black. I want more adults in the museum.

### Participants' Perspectives

1. Jill
Age: forty-six
Education: some college
Occupation: homemaker

I took a friend on these tours for her birthday. She is an organ enthusiast and chose this particular program. I am a musician and love history, though I

*continued*

**CASE STUDY 3.1 (continued)**

didn't know much about organs before taking this course. The guides gave a nice timeline and brochures about the various organs. The main tour guide was a professional organist, so he was familiar with all the organs we visited. I'm on the music committee at my church, and this program has helped me with planning music there.

2. Jane
Age: sixty
Education: postgraduate degree
Occupation: homemaker

At first I thought I wouldn't like this tour, but I decided it would be nice to go with my husband. I also thought it might be good since it included music and local history. I got more than I bargained for. I had very little interest beforehand, but as the tour went on it became more interesting. As I learned more, I wanted to know more.

The best part about the program was developing an appreciation of the organ itself as a piece of art in the beautiful buildings where they were housed. The Organ Crawl led me to analyze how the organ, as a piece of art, is displayed in my own church. The organs did not have to have the biggest sound to be best; some of the small ones sounded sweetest.

3. Joe
Age: seventy-two
Education: some college
Occupation: retired flight manager

My main motivation for attending this program was to meet and get to know other people with similar interests. I am an organ enthusiast and am building an organ at home. I liked the way the program started with the most modern organ and ended with the oldest. I will remember seeing all the organs and hearing them, too. I particularly liked the hands-on aspects of this program. I like to do tours and see specific collections of things (e.g., wildlife, arboretums). A few participants even got to play some of the organs. I liked the fact that we got to meet some of the people who built the organs we saw. We even went to an organ factory. I felt it was very well planned and the guides were very knowledgeable. I really enjoyed the program, though the school buses they used to transport us were very uncomfortable.

**Research Observation**

Handouts were mailed to registrants several days ahead of time. Before participants boarded the bus, tour leaders handed out an additional folder containing information on the organ builders and organ construction. Tour leaders traveled on the bus with the group. An organist was at each stop to provide varied amounts of instruction. The first organist was quite comprehensive, describing the instrument and its major features. She introduced each organ selection and pointed out the special sections. She also gathered participants close to the instrument so they could assist her in pumping and playing. The second organist was very brief with his introduction and instruction. Moreover, he spoke only to those who gathered around the organ, ignoring the rest of the people in the church. The third organist introduced himself, the organ, and the piece, leaning over the choir loft railing to make sure everyone could hear him.

For the final stop, the tour guide was also the organist. His strength as a teacher was the way he formed a relationship with many people on the tour. His comments on the music he played were more casual, even to the point of referring to using some of his aunt's music books.

Much depended on the sites visited and the local organist. The time on the bus provided opportunities to visit and discuss, but none of this was organized or led by the tour guide.

Participants were involved to various degrees. All were involved in moving from place to place. Some were more involved in that they gathered around the organ and visited with the organist between pieces.

Varied levels of knowledge and interest determined the degree to which learners' needs were met. Some were more interested in the bus tour than the organ recitals. The playing of pieces, demonstrations of stops, hand pumping, and opening and closing of shutters all were opportunities for participants to apply and analyze information. Learning at the levels of synthesis and evaluation were also occasionally evident during discussions among participants. The program definitely provided an opportunity for participants to compare organ characteristics and suitability.

### Analysis

The Organ Crawl exemplified several important aspects of successful adult museum programs. In particular, the program was multisensory. Participants heard the music from each organ, saw the organs and the architecture of the buildings they were in, and actually got to play organs or manipulate parts of organs. The social and interactive components of this program were also extremely important. Participants had many opportunities to socialize with each other on the bus or at churches. Participants also felt comfortable asking questions of the main tour guide and of the specific presenters.

The social component of this program was clearly important to the first participant, but she was also motivated by her own interests. She expects to use

*continued*

CASE STUDY 3.1 (*continued*)

what she learned in this program in her work as a member of her church music committee.

The second participant is the prototypical tag-along. She went along because her husband wanted to participate, then she became personally engaged. This participant also experienced "integrative" learning, integrating what she learned into her own life by analyzing how the organ in her own church is displayed.

The third participant indicated that learning through social interaction was his primary motivation for taking this program, though skill building was also important. He was very interested in meeting and speaking with experts in order to help him with his project at home, because he already owned as many books as he could find on organ building. For this participant, access to people (expert organ builders), places (organ factory, churches), and things (organs) made the program a success.

## Planner Perspectives on Choosing, Training, Supporting, and Retaining Adult Education Instructors

### What to Look for in Choosing an Instructor

Program planners look for instructors who can wear at least four hats: programmer (to arrange conditions to facilitate learning); guide (to assist others in their educative experiences); content resource (to serve as the authority in one or more fields of study); and institutional representative (to represent the museum and promote the institution's mission).[1] What does it take to fulfill so many roles? For starters, it takes each of the traits discussed below.

### Experience and Credibility

What gives this person the right to talk about this particular subject or teach this particular class? Experience and credibility may come from a college education or from the school of life. Some program managers require instructors to have professional experience in one of the museum's specialties, such as archaeology, anthropology, zoology, or geology. Checking the past teaching record of prospective instructors may provide more reliable estimates of teaching ability. It is a good practice to interview someone who has hired the instructor in the past to ascertain credibility. All too often, planners do not review an instructor's track record before hiring him or her.

*Credentials*

Some museums only use in-house staff as program leaders, while others exclusively hire instructors from outside the institution. Most tend to use a combination of the two. A curator at one natural history museum reported using "Ph.D. level professors, graduate students, students, faculty from the College of Education, resource agency professionals, and English professors." The education director for a botanic garden looks for "experienced gardeners and craftspeople. An education background is important, but experience is more important." A good practice is to hire contract instructors with a broad array of credentials, accompanied by a positive attitude and shared enthusiasm for teaching. We observed an example of a poor practice at one university museum that typically only employed university faculty as contract instructors. Such practices contribute to a closed system of planners, instructors, and program participants, discouraging audience diversity.

*Teaching Ability and Style*

Program planners want dynamic, engaging teachers who are able to successfully interpret their subject matter for an audience. Advocates of lifelong learning make the best instructors of adults. One educator at a university art museum asks prospective instructors: Have you taught adults before? Are you interactive with people? Do you encourage participation? Are you sensitive to the needs of adults and seniors?

*Good Communication Skills*

Instructors need strong interpersonal communication skills and skills in public speaking. They must be able to communicate with a diversity of people and be able to present ideas in a way that will resonate with a broad audience. One of the most important communication skills is the ability to listen.

*Professionalism and Personality*

Instructors who are professional, flexible, and unflappable make excellent program leaders. Individuals with vibrant personalities and accessible demeanors put participants at ease and infect them with enthusiasm for the subject. Such instructors often demonstrate a real love for teaching and are innovative thinkers and presenters. Best practice suggests conducting personal interviews with instructors and observing them teaching.

*Good museum instructors give from the heart, want to be there, gain as much as they give, and fulfill their own needs as well as those of the museum.*

Anne Mumm, Lied Discovery Children's Museum

*Good instructors have passion, creativity, and the ability to make connections between diverse groups and topics.*

Jessica Arcand, Andy Warhol Museum

*Museum Experience*

Most program planners prefer instructors who have experience working in a museum setting. Such instructors are likely to understand what a museum can offer and are prepared to take advantage of all resources that may serve their programs. Some program managers think in terms of how well an instructor fits within the overall mission of the museum. However, our research team found that a large portion of the instructors we contacted had little or no museum experience. They taught their museum classes in the same manner with the same content in other community settings. To ensure a new instructor shares your vision and has access to museum resources, provide a site tour of resources and a written outline of information you would like them to convey (see appendix A). Offer a regular training program for current and potential instructors to introduce the art of teaching with objects and working with adults.

---

**CASE STUDY 3.2**

**Finding It on the Web, Science Center**

**General Description**

This computer workshop provided an overview of common Web search tools currently available, including Alta Vista, Yahoo, and Lycos. Participants could do simple or complex searches, learn to capture and organize information, and mirror Web pages for use off-line. The workshop was held in the museum's computer lab. Each student had a computer to work on. The instructor's computer was hooked into a projector so all could see his screen. Some Internet experience was required. The course was held on a Saturday, from 10:00 a.m. to 1:00 p.m. Cost was $66.

*continued*

## Institutional Perspective

It is important to make money, but making money can also be a curse. Big money makers are encouraged by museum administration. If you can sell out a program once, they think you can sell it out four times per year. If one program makes money, the expectation is that all programs will make money. I just want to cover costs—that defines a winner to me. I expect fee programs to cover 100 percent of direct and indirect costs.

I want to put on relevant programs and I hope participants will remember that the program was enjoyable and valuable. In some programs I hope that participants will remember the goal set for the course, like a skill learned. Really I want both—that they remember what they learned and that the program was fun.

## Instructor's Perspective

I'm a computer consultant, programmer, and Web-site designer. I teach at the museum through a partnership with the Center for Adult Education, where I have been an instructor for twenty years. I concentrate on the basics. I have taught the course twenty-plus times and I use material that has worked best in the past.

I constantly monitor my approach to teaching and change it as I find better ways to pass the knowledge along. I don't have any previous knowledge of the students, so I poll the class as to their desires and experience at the beginning and then aim for the middle. Museum program participants have a higher than average understanding that life is a learning experience. They like to learn.

I see myself as a repository of knowledge for the students to tap into. I'm a test pilot for software, looking at how it works in the real world for real people.

## Participants' Perspectives

1. Peter
Age: not given
Education: postgraduate degree
Occupation: real-estate broker

I took this class specifically to learn practical information about the Internet. I liked the hands-on experience, the practical information, and just getting ideas. The instructor was well prepared.

2. Sue
Age: twenty-seven
Education: college degree
Occupation: marketing

My goal was to gain a better understanding of searching the Web. I will remember learning about different platforms (Mac and Windows) and different

*continued*

browsers. The instructor used great everyday examples to define terminology. He was very thorough.

I liked that the class was hands-on. The instructor had his own computer terminal and LCD projector and we could follow along on our computers. It was a great way to see and do.

## Observer's Perspective

The instructor immediately developed a good rapport with the early-arriving students. He began the class by answering any questions the students had. This helped him gauge the previous learning level of the class and tailor the program to the students present. Problems with the Internet server access completely changed the course from hands-on to almost purely lecture. Every student was pretty disappointed that they didn't get as much chance to practice searching the net as they wanted to.

The class had the potential to be excellent, but the server problems severely hindered that potential. The instructor was very good. He was enthusiastic, knowledgeable, and dynamic. He did an excellent job, despite the equipment problems. The reference materials handed out were excellent. Every student received a handout and an information-filled computer diskette to take home. Helpful Web sites and programs were regularly presented in the class.

## Analysis

Sometimes the success of a program is beyond control. We often think of weather being a major factor in the success of field trips, but in this instance, technical problems with the on-line connection for the museum's computer lab nearly killed the program. What should have been hands-on, experiential learning turned into a lecture. The instructor said he would have canceled the class if he had known what the on-line connection would be like. Normally the museum is hooked up with an ultrafast Internet connection that greatly facilitates programs like this one. The instructor said that in all the times he had done programs in the museum's computer lab there had never been a problem.

Despite unexpected and uncontrollable problems, programs can still accomplish some of their goals. Participants learned the basics of surfing the Internet and even got some hands-on experience, even though it wasn't at the level that the instructor had hoped for. The key to the success of this program was flexibility. The instructor was faced with an insurmountable barrier in completing his plan for the program. Fortunately, he was flexible enough to carry on. The instructor polled the class prior to beginning in order to assess not only their previous knowledge, but also the direction of their interests. Then despite technical difficulties, he created a program that met the participants' needs.

All museum education directors should seek instructors who are flexible in their lesson plans and comfortable with their abilities. Neither rain, nor mechanical problems, nor a power outage, nor noise, nor getting lost, nor any act of God or other problem should derail the train, yet problems like these are often cited as the main reason for a program failing. Instructors who can adapt and still produce a successful program despite unexpected barriers are priceless.

*Availability*

Plain and simple, are instructors available? Will they work for little or no pay? The founder and director of one small science institute looks for a "willingness to teach for a limited fee. That quality is found only in those who are passionate about their area of expertise." The director of another small natural heritage project admits, "We're pretty opportunistic. We look for someone who fits our overall mission and who has a program that funds itself or [that] with limited funding we can pay for."

## The Role of the Museum in Instructor Training

Very few of the instructors we interviewed had training in adult or continuing education. This unfortunate fact is consistent with other museum studies. Few institutions provide staff development in the area of adult education, so consequently, little effort seems to be given to instructing the instructors. The quality of instructors and instruction would benefit greatly if museum educators shared suggestions on working with adults, designing courses, or devising classroom strategies. A small number of program managers we observed met with prospective instructors before committing classes to them, but generally, these interviews were directed toward physical details rather than teaching techniques.

Only 55 percent of all museums surveyed provided instructor training. Except for docent trainees, few museum instructors had the opportunity to discuss with education directors the mission of the museum or the philosophy of the education department. Communication about the museum's mission and some degree of training in teaching methods could benefit instructors and therefore the museum's overall adult education program. Adults tend to avoid weak instructors, or at least give them poor evaluations (that is, if evaluations are used).

## Ways Program Planners Can Support Their Instructors

Here are some ways program planners can help instructors succeed:

- Help instructors understand how best to reach adult learners. In most cases, adult learning is strongly influenced by the relationship of participant and instructor. Adults accept insights more readily, for example, from someone they know and trust. Introductions are a wonderful tool for establishing trust between an unfamiliar presenter and a new audience. Introductions that reveal presenters as individuals worth listening to and trusting (more than simply listing degrees or positions) can set the scene for learning.

- Inform presenters of the presumed level of participants' knowledge. Local program directors may know more than outside presenters about the knowledge level of audiences. Sharing such information can make for more satisfying learning experiences.

- Help instructors who are not part of the museum staff with incidentals. Offer to make copies, arrange the room, put up a bulletin board, retrieve artifacts from the collection. Many instructors have other commitments. Anything the museum can do to make their job easier will likely improve teaching performance and participant enjoyment.

- Help your own staff members improve their teaching practices. Many museum staff members have had little training in teaching methodology. Their graduate school experience was likely limited to teaching models that, in reality, are rather ineffective in informal adult education classes.

- Provide productive feedback. All good instructors want to know how well they did and how they can improve their presentations. We met teachers who were so desperate for feedback that they developed their own procedures for surveying the class. On the positive side, some museum directors hold training sessions, develop helpful guidelines on teaching adults, or personally contact teachers to ask how teaching is going.

- Inform instructors of emergency procedures. Emergencies can vary from heart attacks to two classes being scheduled at the same time in the same room. At minimum, there should be a list of emergency numbers and procedures.

## HELP!

Of the program planners we interviewed:

- Over 90 percent provided some administrative help in the form of making copies, scheduling participants, collecting money, or setting up rooms.
- 93 percent handled program advertisement and publicity.
- 90 percent provided audiovisual equipment.
- Over 80 percent of science, art, and history museums allowed their instructors access to teaching collections or permanent collections.
- 79 percent of art and history museums provided some type of compensation, compared to 68 percent of science museums.
- 99 percent of art and history museums provided professional staff assistance, compared to 81 percent of science museums. Staff assistance might include helping the instructor in the classroom, running the slide projector during a lecture, or driving a van for a field trip.
- Only 55 percent of all museums surveyed provided instructor training.

## Keeping Good Instructors Once You Have Them

Once you have found those dynamic instructors, how do you hold on to them? First, orient them to the museum. Provide an open house so instructors can meet each other as well as museum staff. Conduct a tour of the facility, provide a handout answering frequently asked questions, offer information about student evaluation and performance expectations, and let them know of any handbooks, newsletters, mailing lists, social events, or special meetings that may be of interest.[2]

Make instructors feel they are part of the museum family. Pair new instructors with full-time staff members who will act as coaches or mentors. Provide ongoing feedback so instructors know how they are doing; point out areas in which they succeed and areas in which they can improve. Encourage instructors to take part in staff meetings and professional and curriculum development activities. Provide incentives or rewards such as tuition benefits, travel costs, or vouchers for other programs.

## Barriers to Successful Adult Programs

Not surprisingly, when we asked program planners about the obstacles to their success, many of them reflected the universal struggles of museum educators: "We need better funding, . . . more volunteer help, . . . larger audiences, . . . more classroom space." As the manager of adult education and technical services at a natural history museum put it, "Always—money, time, and staff." The good news is, such answers show a clear desire for expanding and improving adult programs.

### Money

Without sufficient funds, many museums cannot afford to provide adult programs, since their limited resources are often reserved for children's programming. Also, when money is tight, programs suffer from compromises in instruction, tools, and materials.

In our survey, we asked if adult education programs were required to make money. Approximately a third of respondents said no. Another third were required to at least break even. The remaining third said that money played a major role in the types of adult programming they could offer, so programs had to make money.

### Staffing

Although not true of all education departments, many are understaffed, considering the number of events and programs they provide. "Staffing is our number one problem, more than money. Right now we have only two full-time people," said one director. Coworkers in other departments can't always stop what they're doing to help set up a room for a lecture or move equipment for a workshop, or stay until the end of a class to lock the building. Many adult programs are offered on evenings or weekends to accommodate participants' work schedules. With limited staff to set up, tear down, and supervise, this can lead to unwanted overtime for museum education staff and to possible burnout.

### Facilities

How can a museum hold a seminar for one hundred people when their auditorium only accommodates twenty-five? How can a class or workshop succeed in an auditorium without tables? How can a lecture, class, and teacher workshop be given on the same Saturday with only two museum spaces available? As the curator at one county museum said, "Space is our number one problem. We have no meeting room. More people sign up for programs than we can handle, so we end up with waiting lists."

Many of the museums that we visited had classrooms and auditoriums that were simply inadequate for adult programs. Seating was uncomfortable, desks or tables were lacking or not stable, where lighting was poor, and where sound systems were nonexistent. While it is true that some of these facilities were developed before adult programs became popular, the message to adult participants is that they are unimportant to the museum. Adults do not demand state-of-the-art facilities, but they do appreciate comfortable learning environments that do not distract them from the task at hand.

Program planners are continually on the lookout for places to hold programs and events. Even large museums may have space issues. For example, the Los Angeles County Museum of Art offers a teacher workshop for hundreds of local teachers. The workshop includes several lectures, workshops, dramatic presentations, and gallery demonstrations all in one evening. Finding enough space for all of the activities and teachers is a challenge, but with cooperative planning and an eye on all spaces indoors and out, the program continues to grow.

Besides space considerations, the location of the museum itself may be a barrier to successful programming. Unsafe neighborhoods, inconvenient parking, and poor lighting can all deter a potential audience. Look at the location you plan to use for the program. Is it available, accessible, and comfortable? What is the parking situation? The place should be consistent with the program design, audience, and budget and with the museum's image. Does the physical setting environment portray a positive image for the museum? Some programs may need to be offered at a certain facility because of equipment needs or availability, but is the facility accessible? Are there alternative locations available in case of poor weather or technical difficulties? (On the flip side, Rosemary Caffarella warns about letting the location "outshine" the program.)

## Marketing and Promotion

People can't come to a program if they don't know about it. As the education director of one nature and science center lamented, "We don't know how to market our programs. We need to let adults know what we do." A better understanding of marketing principles and techniques can help programmers reach their target audience—indeed, can help programmers discover who their target audiences are. Most program planners could benefit from a workshop on marketing, perhaps through the informal learning network of which they are a part. (See chapter 6 for marketing tips.)

## Increased Competition

Many organizations are vying for adults' precious leisure time. As the docent coordinator at a large natural history museum remarked, "There is so much for people to do and not enough time to do it all. Even within the museum, many different programs are going on at the same time." Programs must be of the highest quality if they are to continually draw participants who have so much to choose from. Some museum managers avoid competing with other community groups by working with those entities to build cooperative programs that benefit all involved, especially the adult learner.

In many museums, educators need to find creative ways to work more effectively with the marketing department to ensure good marketing external to the museum. They also need to be the catalysts in helping other departments that work with adults (e.g., volunteer and docent training, teacher training, curatorial departments) to ensure that adult programs are effectively marketed internally.

## Scheduling

Because of work schedules, many adult participants can only attend programs offered in the evenings or on weekends, although programs scheduled during the noon hour are proving popular at some places. The early evening, from 5:30 P.M. to 6:30 P.M., is a convenient time for those who like to attend programs after work but before heading home. Later start times may serve adults who have to go home to tend family needs in the early evening before going back out, but may not work for older adults who don't like to drive at night.

## Diverse Audience Needs

Not understanding what an audience wants or needs was repeatedly mentioned as a barrier to a successful program. Not all museum classes or programs are a rousing success, and in some cases, individual program participants disliked aspects of a program so much that they told us that *they hated the program.* Once again the importance of the instructor comes through in participants' complaints about museum programs. The way the instructor presented his or her material was the largest cause of displeasure among program participants.

*"The content of this speaker's talk was not very original. He covered many of the same things as the first speaker."*

Program participant, art museum speaker series

*"The entire class was spent on how to grow flowers from seedlings. I hoped to learn more about which hearty perennials would grow in my backyard."*

Program participant, botanical garden

*"The lecture lacked a central theme. The instructor tended to let his lecture wander rather than staying on the subject."*

Program participant, natural history museum

*"Unfortunately, the vocabulary was dumbed down and the instructor sometimes spoke down to the class."*

Program participant, natural history museum

*"The lecture was somewhat overwhelming. It was a little too advanced and specific. I'd like to see more how-to classes that relate to exhibits in the museum."*

Program participant, science center

Program participants also were often critical of the instructor's personality or teaching style. Some program participants said the instructor was an expert on the subject matter, but a bad teacher. Many of these issues can be mitigated with more careful selection of contract instructors combined with being restrictive regarding which instructor's contracts are renewed. Sometimes problems can be mitigated with more clearly defined program descriptions. Other issues related to diverse audience needs, however, cannot be easily resolved given the individual nature of learner needs. Sometimes in order to protect the program, you will have to restrict adults with unrealistic expectations from participating in a course.

## Other Barriers

There are more intractable issues, such as a museum director without vision, organizational systems that do not encourage teamwork or cooperation, an inherited program structure, other institutional priorities, other departmental priorities, a disengaged board of trustees, internal regulations, and poor facilities.

Program planners must make choices about issues they can change to achieve excellence and others they cannot. Like everything in life, their compromise must be made in terms of time, energy, and resources. Pick your battles. Program planners can control most of the variables that are the foundation for excellent programs. They can establish the mission and vision for adult programs, set a tone for excellence, invest in adult education training for staff, carefully hire and train instructors, support the efforts of the marketing department, and make the best possible use of museum resources.

## New Perspectives

Where you have more intractable issues, choose to be a leader for change. For example, invite board members and local media to participate in programs. Create a personal advisory board for programs. Good community "buzz" can help build program advocates. When enough staff can get together and recommit themselves to a shared vision, anything is possible.

At the end of our study, we were encouraged to see that adult lives were changing as a result of excellent programs in museums. Program planners are at the heart of this. In the best situations, guidance from planners helped position instructors and museum educators to help adults explore their worlds. How and where this is most successfully accomplished is the focus of the next chapter, on instructors.

## Notes

1. Roger Hiemstra, "The State of the Art," in *Selected Reprints from Museums, Adults and the Humanities: A Guide for Educational Programming* (Washington, D.C.: American Association of Museums, 1993), 47.

2. M. Bankirer, "Adjunct Faculty as Integrated Resources in Continuing Education," in *Organization and Administration of Continuing Education: A Textbook Designed to Facilitate Successful Programs and Processes in Adult and Continuing Education,* ed. V. W. Mott and L. C. Rampp (Checotah, Okla.: AP Publications, 1995), 139.

# CHAPTER FOUR

# THE INSTRUCTORS

Teaching's not telling. It's motivating people to learn.

—Program instructor

Two natural history museums in the Midwestern United States offered an astronomy lecture about the same time of year with nearly identical material. Both were medium-sized institutions with similar facilities and the two participant groups were quite similar. The only appreciable difference between the two programs was the instructors. Participants walking away from one lecture appeared bored and dissatisfied. One was heard to say, "Who did that guy think we were? He was more interested in impressing us with his language than teaching." Another person leaving the auditorium complained about the dull and monotonous delivery. In contrast, the audience walking away from the other lecture appeared energized. "That was exciting!" one woman exclaimed to her companion. " What challenging ideas!"

No doubt about it, instructors can make or break a program. Many of the program planners we interviewed insisted that the instructor was the most important part of any museum program. Over 90 percent of the participants surveyed agreed that a program's success hinged on having a dynamic, well-organized instructor. As we traveled across the country, we confirmed this assessment, observing instructors who made less-appealing topics exciting and instructors who made exciting topics mundane or incomprehensible.

This chapter examines the role of the instructor and explores the whys and hows, the joys and problems of teaching adults in the museum setting.

*Students learn about tropical plants in the Missouri Botanical Garden's Climatron® from instructor John MacDougal.* (Courtesy Missouri Botanical Garden.)

## Anatomy of an Instructor

What makes a good adult museum instructor?[1] According to adult education expert Alan Knox, effective teaching is a combination of content mastery and teaching style. Good instructors are responsive, respect and understand their students' needs, provide learning options for individuals as well as the group, and select appropriate materials.[2] Perhaps the most important aspect of effective teaching is the relationship between teacher and learner.[3] So good instructors must know what they're talking about and be able to engage their audience.

> *I want to get people excited, and knowledge is the tool to do that. I try to deliver knowledge in small quantities, because there is only so much people can absorb at once. . . . When you teach algebra, you expect them to learn about it, but they don't go out on weekends looking for algebra problems. Give them enough knowledge to direct their enthusiasm.*
>
> Contract instructor

Who are these interesting and engaging instructors? Where do they come from? The majority of museum instructors we interviewed were highly educated and typically held a master's degree. This is not surprising, considering the general museum adult participant is also highly educated. For a lecture series, a museum might draft international or local "celebrities" or professors from area universities. Artists, historians, and scientists are good candidates for teaching technical classes, while community volunteers and retired teachers often serve as tour guides. Many individuals turn a hobby into a museum teaching career, using their enthusiasm for a topic to spark the interest of others. A significant number of the instructors we interviewed had business experience related to the subject they taught. This type of professional background seemed to appeal to learners.

Among the museum instructors we interviewed, 40 percent had taught the same program before, 43 percent had taught other programs in the museum setting, and 71 percent had taught the same program in other settings, such as adult education programs, Elderhostel, or community clubs. Teaching experience ranged from four months to thirty-four years, with an average of twelve-and-one-half years.

*People enjoy my storytelling style and seem to like my lively presentations. Stories that reflect our local area are especially popular. People unfamiliar with local flavor enjoy that type of thing. A lot of people come in thinking that history is boring and dull, and one of my goals is to make history fun and lively. I want them to have a good time. Learning history should be as much fun as going to an amusement park. It just needs to be presented correctly.*

Contract instructor

While museums must often seek out and recruit tour guides or docents, they don't generally have to advertise for instructors, because so many people are interested in teaching at a museum. Program managers may simply request course outlines from individuals they believe might fit into the program.

### Self-Made Models

Unfortunately, few museums provide instructors with training in adult education (see chapter 3). In the absence of museum-provided training, instructors are left to their own devices in modeling their teaching approaches. Consider these instructor comments:

"I mostly model myself after the five staff members I work with, each of whom has a different teaching style. I try to copy the best points of each."

"I model after John Dobson. He would drag telescopes around the main streets of San Francisco and set them up so that the ordinary citizen could look at the sky. Another role model for me was Carl Sagan, because of the way he talked. He made astronomy popular, he never talked over people's heads, and he made it accessible."

"I have modeled my teaching after fifty years of university life, including my undergraduate and graduate training. One of my undergraduate professors was especially influential on my own teaching style. This professor allowed people to discover things on their own. He may have set up the circumstances, but then he would gently guide them to their own discovery. He used a light-handed approach, with a sense of collegiality and a shared sense of mutual discovery."

"I don't model on anyone. But from what I've seen, I know what *not* to do."

"In general, I follow the approach I take in the college classroom, using overhead transparencies and the chalkboard. I would have spent less time on the lecture, although that was what I was asked to do. I did what I was asked to do rather than what I would have preferred to do."

"I have modeled my teaching after some of the best teachers I knew, who involved the participants and got them excited. I'm there to provide knowledge and to serve as a resource person. My main job is to get people excited."

## The Key Role of Instructors, as They See It

The instructors we interviewed had varying views of their roles as teachers of adults, although the overwhelming majority shared the same sincere commitment to the learning process. As instructors' comments suggest, they have several main roles.

### Facilitate Learning

"I feel I am more of a facilitator. I like to give people an opportunity to explore and expand what they know about a subject. I don't think of myself as knowing more than them, but as having a different set of understandings.

I try to teach students how to find their own answers. I am not a one-way conduit of knowledge. I like participants to share their knowledge as well."

"Good facilitators open visual and intellectual doors. They help people learn how to really see and encourage them to open their eyes to gain deeper understanding."

### Convey a Sense of Fun, Excitement, and Confidence

"I want to make learning fun. I use a lot of humor to give a lighter tone to the class. In my classes, I encourage interaction between participants and emphasize that there are no wrong answers."

"As a teacher, I am responsible for getting people enthusiastic about whatever subject I am teaching. If I have failed to do so, then I have not taught them anything. For example, if after my class on butterflies people do not even turn their heads when seeing a butterfly, I know I have failed to teach them anything."

### Attend to Participants

"I come in early and set up the chairs, then go around and personally invite people to come for the guided tour. The tour is announced over the public address system, but I find that if I go up to people personally I get a larger group. I tell them that there will be seats. If you've been in the museum for awhile, you're ready to sit down."

"It is easy for an instructor to make an audience think he is smart. It is much more challenging to make the audience feel that *they* are smart."

### Encourage Active, Hands-On Participation

"For piquing interest in a topic, the more hands-on activities the better. It is important to tie the class and materials to everyday life. My role is to give participants as much evidence as possible to work with."

"Realism and interaction with objects are very important and help make the class more authentic."

## Characteristics of Successful Instructors

What do directors of museum educational programs look for in adult program instructors? In our interviews with museum program planners, we

CASE STUDY 4.1

**Botanic Gardens**

**Reflections of an Instructor**

I've been a professional floral designer for thirty-eight years. I became associated with the botanical gardens after I called them for a business-related question. After our conversation, the education director asked me to come up with a prospectus for teaching courses. My initial goal was to become a more skillful teacher, which I feel I've accomplished.

Teaching is more than just knowing your subject. It is bonding with your students, giving significant praise, and helping students achieve their goals. I want to engage class participants in the art of floral arranging and help them find the rewards of discovering their own style and philosophy, without getting hung up on the technical aspects.

I always start my classes with a discussion in which participants share what they want to make and why. Then I use that information to help them develop the skills to "make clear a philosophy in aesthetic experience." Many inspirational books on flower arranging are available, however they can be discouraging, because they show the work of professional designers. As a result, many people get the sense that flower arranging is too difficult—that it's something they can't do when actually this is a very forgiving art form.

In my classes, the student first learns how simple an art form this is. I stress that it is not what you have created, but whether *what* you have created has *spiritual meaning* to you. You have to have a vision and follow through on making that vision happen. But you can't have a vision until you know what you like.

Flower arranging makes the rewards of gardening a year-round affair. It helps people focus and isolate individual flowers for their arranging value (color, texture, general botany, and other factors). Flower arranging allows the students a more personal experience with the plants.

**Reflections of a Program Participant**

We were all nervous as we began our flower-arranging class, but our instructor had a way of making light comments which made all of us feel at ease. He seemed genuinely interested in his subject. Not being particularly creative, I thought this class would be a challenge.

First we learned the different flowers commonly used in arrangements. We learned that there are various types of arrangements and that arrangements

*continued*

typically contain a variety of flower sizes, colors, textures, and heights. I tend to try to get the "right arrangement," so learning that there wasn't one correct technique took a lot of pressure off me.

I put a Styrofoam mounting block into my pot and began inserting some of the flowers. It was amazing how many ideas I got from watching and working with some of the other class members. When I had completed about a third of my arrangement, I asked the instructor for comments. With his usual humorous style, he suggested moving some of the flowers around and adding grasses and ferns. The best part of the class was taking something home I had created myself.

discovered several recurring qualities common to good instructors. We list them here in order of their importance to program planners and share some composite comments about each characteristic. These cited qualities were quite similar to the qualities adult education expert Rosemary Caffarella identifies as characteristic of good instructors of adults.[4]

## Knowledge of Subject Matter

"Instructors should have expertise in the subject area. Those who thoroughly understand their subjects know how to make their topic relevant to individual audiences and can make their presentations come alive."

## Teaching Ability or Competence

"The best instructors love to teach and have the ability to communicate well with students and work with a wide range of student learners. Quality instructors adjust their teaching methods to the learner's needs and genuinely care that the participants learn. They open themselves to the audience and know who the audience is."

## Enthusiasm and Commitment

"Good museum instructors give from the heart, want to be there, gain as much as they give, and fulfill their own needs as well as those of the museum. They have passion, creativity, and the ability to make connections between diverse groups and topics."

## Personal Effectiveness

"Instructors should be organized, prepared, stable, responsible, adaptable, and exhibit a 'spark' for learning. The best instructors have a sense of humor and respect participants' experiences and perspectives."

## Communication and Public-Speaking Skills

"Instructors should be able to communicate their subject at the appropriate audience level; no scholarly performance is required. Good instructors have the ability to relate to audiences and hold their attention. Such instructors are generally excellent public presenters, able to talk to an informed and interested lay audience without lapsing into scholarly performance."

*"The Geologic History and Stream Dynamics of Bighorn Canyon."The instructor, Larry French, is using a Brunton compass while students look on.* (Courtesy Western Heritage Center.)

## The Instructor's Toolbox

Adult learners know what they want to explore and how they want to go about it. The instructor is a facilitator in this process. However, this does not mean instructors should ignore teaching methods or content mastery. As Alan Knox points out, a deep understanding of the subject is vital, because it allows instructors to relate content to the interests of participants and help participants deal with underlying value judgments.[5]

Adult educator Stephen Brookfield warns that the concept of "facilitator of learning" exercises something of a "conceptual stranglehold on our notions of correct educational practice."[6] The problem with accepting facilitation as the sum total of the educator's responsibility is that it assumes that the learner possesses a high degree of self-knowledge and critical awareness. "To act as a resource person to adults who are unaware of belief systems, bodies of knowledge, or behavioral possibilities other than those that they have uncritically assimilated since childhood," says Brookfield, "is to condemn such adults to remaining with existing paradigms of thought and action."[7]

Thus it appears that, to be a truly effective instructor, educators of adults need to be competent in several areas. They must understand not only how adults learn, but also how life experiences may have influenced an individual's knowledge or opinions. They must have a comprehensive and insightful understanding of their subject. And they should have a clear mission for their instructional program, whether that mission is to entertain, inform, or develop life-changing attitudes or skills.

Here are fourteen ways program planners can help instructors deliver a successful learning experience:

- Secure a comfortable and clean teaching space.

- Work with the instructor to provide participants with a course overview in advance. Put it on your Web site.

- Acquire information about participants' needs and interests for the instructor.

- Provide equipment, supplies, and teaching resources.

- Have a staff person on hand to introduce participants to each other and the instructor.

- Have a staff person handle all final registration and course logistics.

- Encourage the instructor to provide an overview at the beginning of the course.

- Make sure the instructor plans to get participants involved through dialogue or activities.

- Encourage the instructor to set aside time for participants to reflect on what they have learned.

- Provide an evaluation form that solicits useful feedback for the instructor (see appendix C).

- Make sure participants know how to contact you to provide feedback.

- Be available to address instructor and participant needs.

- Review the course with the instructor.

- Write up profile notes on instructor and participants for use in future planning.

Four additional tips for instructors come from an experienced contract instructor:

1. Publicize, Publicize, Publicize! Don't be afraid to advertise several hundred miles away. People will come if they are interested.

2. Arrive early, get set up, then greet people as they come through the door. Folks like a handshake, a friendly question.

3. Believe in the power of narrative. People remember learning through story. It's much better than throwing facts at them. Always use humor!

4. Always, always end with a question session! Most people come to a program with an agenda; they have questions which they want answered, so always leave time to answer these questions.

## The Instructor's Guide to Basic Learning Models

No matter how experienced your instructors are, most have probably not given much thought to how adults learn in informal situations. Let instructors know there are three generally recognized methods of organizing learning experiences: teacher directed, learner centered, and collaborative.[8]

Most people imagine the teacher-directed mode when they think of learning. In this case, the teacher is seen as having responsibility for planning learning experiences, selecting materials, and setting goals and objectives.

In a learner-centered environment, the student actively participates in creating and directing the learning experience. The teacher serves as a facilitator who provides resources and ideas. Adult educator Malcolm Knowles advocates the learner-centered approach to teaching adults.

In the collaborative mode, the teacher's primary responsibility is to facilitate student learning by letting the student set the direction and accept responsibility for it. Paulo Freire's model for education is based on the collaborative approach.[9] He regards the teacher as a facilitator who stimulates learning through dialogue, rather than as the embodiment of knowledge.

Among these three broad approaches, the learner-centered and collaborative modes are usually considered to be the most effective with adults. However, all learners and learning situations are unique. Instructors can judge the circumstances to determine which approach will work best for any given situation.

What participants told us about their learning preferences supports the approach described by Knowles of mutual trust and mutual responsibility. Participants see instructors or resource persons as fellow learners and accept responsibility for their learning; they are not afraid to take initiative.[10]

---

CASE STUDY 4.2

*Flintknapping: Buffalo Museum of Science*

**General Description**

This six-week course taught the basics of chipping arrowheads and spear points from chert, better known as flint. All equipment and materials were provided. The course was limited to ten students and ran from

*continued*

## CASE STUDY 4.2 (continued)

7:00 p.m. to 9:00 p.m. A field trip was arranged with the class. Ages thirteen and up were accepted. The cost was $40 for members, $48 for nonmembers.

### Institutional Perspective

I hope for diverse programs and happy participants. Education is the important thing. I hope classes are enjoyable, put no pressure on participants, and are not overwhelming, and that participants meet people, make friends, and learn something, too. Classes need to meet a financial bottom line, but if class fees cover instructor and security costs, that's okay. The onus is really on the development department to raise money. We'd rather do a class for only four people than turn four people away.

Naturally, I require instructors to be accurate with the information given to course participants, but I leave content up to them and let them determine what will work and what won't. A good instructor makes for a good program. I will, however, work more closely with an instructor after negative feedback.

Our biggest barrier is a lack of support from the museum administration and marketing departments. The new format for the educational offerings brochure is confusing. People can't envision the programs because the descriptions are poor. The brochure format is destroying the education department. People need a good description of the class and want to know how long a class is and who the instructor is.

Adults like hands-on activities. Adults like to take something home with them; it helps make the experience more tangible. Also, program planners and instructors need to be more aware of issues relating to seniors. For one, health issues are important when working with seniors. Also, seniors are more interested in the social aspects of the programs and want more pampering, although they are also very active learners.

### Instructor's Perspective

My interest in flintknapping began in 1991, when I started collecting artifacts. I did some research on the artifacts and joined a couple of local archaeological clubs, where I met experts in the field. One of these experts was associated with the Buffalo Museum of Science. One thing led to another and I began teaching the flintknapping class. I enjoy the subject and like the chance to earn some money.

*continued*

I have taught similar one-day courses for local archaeological and historical clubs, nature clubs, craft guilds, Boy Scouts, and such. Usually, I don't know anything about the class participants ahead of time. Occasionally, participants from the one-day courses sign up for a six-week course. I've even had some participants in my class whom I met over the Internet or at local clubs, where I told them about the course.

I don't expect the participants to be making arrowheads by the end of the course. But I would like participants to take away an understanding of the process involved in flintknapping and to develop an appreciation of what pre-historic peoples had to go through in using this process.

The greatest constraint I deal with is participants' lack of basic knowledge of the subject coming into the class. I have a book I use and sell during the class for interested individuals. In some ways, it would be helpful if the participants read this book prior to starting the class. Most participants start at square one. I provide the materials, techniques, and tools. I often hear from the participants, "It is a lot harder than you make it look."

What would I do differently next time? Well, the stone chips are pretty sharp and most everyone cuts themselves, so I guess I would bring more Band-Aids.

## Participants' Perspectives

1. Joe
Education: some college
Age: sixty-eight
Occupation: retired

I wanted to experience flintknapping and see how arrowheads are made. I generally like hands-on programs with good instructors. I once attended a weekend program at the museum on flintknapping and really enjoyed it because there was a lot of variety.

The instructor was very knowledgeable about his subject, but wasn't exactly the best instructor. I have noticed with other programs that instructors are often experts in their fields, but aren't necessarily good teachers. I don't know whether this was the case in the flintknapping class because I really was the only "greenhorn" in the class; everyone else seemed to have some prior experience with the subject.

Being the only true beginner, I felt frustrated. It was the first time in my life that I can remember that I couldn't do something. There wasn't enough time in the class to ask questions and I was too embarrassed to ask many questions in front of the whole class because I wasn't familiar enough with the subject.

*continued*

**CASE STUDY 4.2 (*continued*)**

This particular program showed me how little I know about a lot of things. I felt frustrated and had trouble with this program because I wasn't prepared ahead of time, but I'm not quite sure how I could've prepared for this program.

**2. Greg**
Education: college graduate
Age: fifty-two
Occupation: electronics

I remember the presentation of how the local Native Americans used tools, and I remember the tie-in of what was happening on other continents as far as the history of tools are concerned.

In this particular class, I liked the fact that there were quite a few experienced amateurs. They added to the class by sharing their knowledge of local history regarding Native Americans and tools. The combination of the expertise of the instructor and the tool expert from the museum with the class members' knowledge was nice.

I'm interested in any science-related adult education courses. I am a member of the museum and this is one of the few adults-only courses the museum offers. Most of the so-called adult courses are family oriented.

**Observer's Perspective**

I observed the second in a series of six classes on flintknapping. The instructor began with a brief lecture and demonstration of techniques, then the course participants practiced on their own as the instructor moved from person to person to offer one-on-one help.

In effect, this program had two instructors. Another instructor who had previously taught the class joined the main instructor. The main instructor did the lectures and demonstrations and moved rapidly from student to student to offer personal assistance. The second instructor would camp next to an individual or a couple of people and work with them intensively for twenty minutes at a time. Together, they made a great instructional team. The use of a teaching assistant like this could work well for many types of museum classes. This way, people who needed more help could get it while others wouldn't feel ignored.

Watching the participants' skills and understanding progress through the evening was fascinating. At first, there was just a constant clatter, as the group

*continued*

seemed to be aimlessly pounding rocks together. After a while, however, the students started developing some skill, and we could all hear when the correct technique was being used. From across the room, participants would remark to each other, "Ooooh, that one sounded good."

**Analysis**

What is *your* analysis of this course? What are its strengths? What are its weaknesses? How could it be improved?

## The Instructor's Touch: Making Programs Meaningful

### Find Out What Participants Want

One of the best ways to make a program meaningful is to ask participants what they want, so many adult educators conduct needs or interest surveys before classes begin. This doesn't have to be a formal or tedious task, as illustrated by the following example:

The museum's director of education contacted me about teaching a blacksmithing course and I agreed to do it because I wanted to do something different and it sounded fun.

The director gave me a list of the participants ahead of time, some of whom I already knew. I contacted the people I didn't know and planned an evening together, so I could ask everyone about their prior experience and what they wanted to achieve. Based on this get-together, I decided what type of projects would be most appropriate.

My own goal was to have participants gain an understanding of blacksmithing at the turn of the century and learn some basic operations on the forge. I wanted everyone to have a chance to make something and make it well. People were so excited to work with hot iron and actually make something. I didn't get any evaluation forms from the museum, so at the end of the summer I met again with participants and asked for feedback on the class.

My schooling in adult education has helped me change my teaching style. Instead of doing lectures, I try to create a participatory group-learning environment: "Get out of their way and let them learn." In this program, I was the facilitator. The majority of participants were older than I and had more knowledge of the farm. I brought up topics which then inspired discussion. I took the role of leading participant.

## Orient and Engage

Orienting a group of adults to the learning task and making them feel at ease are very important. Adults may be uncomfortable gathering with strangers and entrusting their time to a leader they may never have met. "What am I getting myself into?" they wonder. "Should I trust this leader? Will these other people jump on me if I open my mouth? I don't want to look stupid. What are we going to do anyway? How long is it going to take?" Many instructors use humor and introductions to deal with these unvocalized questions. Some begin a learning session with an informal discussion. In this way, instructors develop a feel for the group and establish some rapport A member of our research team observed a good example of this.

*On a perfect summer evening, eighteen adults met on the front porch of an old house for a class on astronomy. Several people knew each other, though most participants were unacquainted. When the instructor, a man in his late forties, arrived the group immediately recognized his easygoing style and began to relax. Introductions took up the first several minutes. As people introduced themselves, it became clear that this was not a "rehearsed group processing activity," but rather an authentic expression of an instructor wanting to get to know his students.*

*After introductions, the instructor gave an overview of what the sky would look like that night. Explanations were kept simple so that everyone in the group could easily understand what was being said. By this time, it was getting dark, so the group took to the porch "observatory" to begin the adventure. The instructor moved from telescope to telescope, answering questions, realigning scopes, and generally making everyone feel at ease. He acknowledged every question as important, often saying "That's a very good question," and gave meaningful answers. Even with advanced questions, he formulated answers the group could understand, then followed up with the questioner on a one-to-one basis. All learners were made to feel important just by the personality of the instructor and his easygoing style.*

## Encourage Active Participation

Hands-on learning was very popular with the majority of museum participants that we interviewed. Instructors agreed on the importance of such learning, though the term "hands-on" had rather broad implications. For many, it seemed to mean some form of active learning rather than manual manipulation of physical material.

*Susan Ahalt, of Ironsides Bird Rescue in Cody, Wyoming, holds Buster the red-tailed hawk while participants sketch, sculpt, or ask questions about her avian charges. This program was held at the National Museum of Wildlife Art in conjunction with the* Wildlife Art for a New Century *exhibition.* (Courtesy National Museum of Wildlife Art.)

The instructor's preparedness and sensitivity to the group's needs directly affects the participants' sense of being active and responsible. Adults value their time; they hate to sit around doing nothing while an instructor decides what to do or searches for material he may have left at home. And spending time with individual students is great, as long as others don't feel neglected.

By employing certain devices, even adults listening to a lecture can be active and involved. Posing rhetorical questions, for example, can stimulate intellectual response. Offering options or alternative positions, especially when presented by more than one speaker, prompts listeners to make decisions and choices. Discussion groups following a presentation, or question-and-answer sessions before, during, or after a presentation, also tend to increase active participation.

With small groups of adults, it is possible to create what Don Seaman and Robert Fellenz call "action" and "interaction" strategies—teaching activities that require active learner participation.[11] Action strategies include simulation games, role playing, and case-study analysis. Interaction strategies include discussions, participatory training, committees, and "buzz" groups. These strategies set the teacher as a facilitator and, in order to be successful, require participants to take part in the learning experience.

## Create a Supportive Atmosphere

Participants' goals and the way an instructor helps learners meet those goals affect the atmosphere of a program. The best instructors create a supportive atmosphere in which adults don't feel threatened by the instructor or other participants. A challenging situation is fine, but a situation that feels threatening distracts attention from learning. The orientation to a session can have a large impact on the atmosphere of the program, both in setting a group at ease and in giving the instructor a feel for the participants.

## Mutual Trust, Mutual Responsibility

As Malcolm Knowles puts it, the ideal adult learning situation—particularly in terms of transformative learning—creates a sense of mutual trust and responsibility. Participants see instructors or resource persons as fellow learners and accept responsibility for their learning; they are not afraid to take the initiative.[12]

The following are suggestions for promoting this sense of mutual responsibility and trust:

- Provide opportunities for participants to prepare for programs. Engaged learners appreciate the opportunity to prepare. The museum or instructor might arrange to have newspaper articles published, mail materials to enrollees, or make relevant information available at the front desk or museum store. Thoughtful introductions to learning events are also helpful. These may go beyond the general orientation (which should be part of every event) to detail the importance of a particular session to an overall program.

- Adjust scheduling and timing of programs to the needs of the participants. This can be accomplished more readily with small groups, but attention to individual and community concerns can make program attendance more convenient for participants. Avoid forcing people to choose between the program and a traditional community event or family celebration. Schedule programs for times of day that are appropriate to the audience and ensure they begin and end on time. Starting and ending late can frustrate and anger participants.

- Provide for social interaction among participants. Small-group interaction can be encouraged by an intimate arrangement of chairs, discussion breaks, or a coffeepot or cookie tray around which the group can gather. In large groups, orientation sessions or dividing participants into smaller groups can encourage social interaction. Name tags are good tools, as are advance lists of attendees. Make time for introductions that include more than name and address. One museum instructor we observed asked each participant for his or her name and a question. In responding, he gave valued information, set the group at ease with his humor, and encouraged interaction as well as learning.

## Barriers Facing Instructors

The job of the adult educator comes with an array of challenges. The obstacles that came up in our interview with instructors run the gamut from poor communication to ill-prepared participants. Recognizing barriers is the first step to breaking them down.

### Communication

Our research team heard an interesting story about one popular instructor who had taught at a museum every year for five years. After one summer class, the program planner expressed to him her concern that his classes were always held in the basement, never in the museum. The instructor was surprised. He thought the museum and collections were off-limits to his students and that bringing his class into the museum would disrupt museum visitors. He had deliberately isolated the class from the museum collections, while the museum program planner preferred that instructors use the museum and its resources. Museum personnel and instructors are busy people, but neglecting communication leads to problems or, at the very least, can impair the quality of programs.

### Facilities

Small rooms and uncomfortable chairs can make it difficult for instructors to conduct classes. Many museums use folding chairs because of their low cost and storage convenience, yet such chairs are not the most suitable for adult participants. Other facilities-related obstacles include a lack of handicap access, inadequate parking, and the location of the museum in an unsafe neighborhood.

## Time

Time—instructor's time, clock time, and museum time—was often cited as a barrier to presenters. Some instructors did not have time to go to the museum beforehand to gather resources or materials. Others felt their class would work better at a different time of the year, but the museum's scheduling made this impossible. Several wanted more time in their individual classes to examine topics in greater depth or to answer questions.

## Institutional Support

Some instructors felt a lack of support from the museum. They thought staff wasn't letting them know what resources were available and felt short-changed in terms of technical support and equipment. Some instructors found that interdepartmental disagreements over equipment and resources made it difficult to conduct their classes.

*Just assembling, transporting, and setting up materials takes four or five hours. It would be easier if I were a full-time instructor, but I have other professional responsibilities as well.*

Contract instructor

*I would like to offer the lawn-care class in the spring, before people have planned their yards, but the course is held in the summer.*

Instructor

*If the museum wants instructors to promote their programs, the development staff needs to do a better job of informing us about the museum's mission and upcoming events and programs.*

Contract instructor

*Instructors need to be funded better. I finally bought my own laptop computer.*

Instructor

## Participants

Occasionally, class participants themselves are viewed as barriers. Participants arrive ill prepared or with unreasonably high expectations for the course. Also, a group may specifically ask that certain objects not be viewed because of religious, political, or social reasons.

## Programs

A few instructors felt that the costs of some programs were too high and that the number of programs offered by the museum was limited. An instructor teaching an introductory class might feel that not having additional classes in that subject area could be a barrier. Some instructors felt that better follow through in programs would lead to more classes for the museum and also a larger knowledge base for students on that particular subject.

## Lack of Publicity

Many instructors felt that courses were drawing a small, repeat segment of the community and so should be more widely publicized. They felt institutions might reach a new audience by displaying posters in feed stores, pet stores, plant nurseries, antique stores, and other targeted spots. A museum art class might attract students by sending a flyer to the local college art-education methods class.

## Instructors and Program Planners as Barriers

When instructors were asked about obstacles to presenting effective programs, none mentioned their own teaching strategies or methods. This may have been due to the nature of the research question or to the fact that museum instructors may not receive feedback on their teaching methods. Or it may be due to the reality that we human beings rarely recognize our own limitations. Since participants in adult classes list the instructor as the most important component in a quality program, instructors may want to focus on self-improvement as at least one achievable goal in breaking down the barriers to effective and successful programs. This is another reason why instructors are encouraged to always use class evaluations.

The same applies to program managers. Much can be learned not only from course evaluations, but from instructors' perceptions of barriers. For example, for the instructor hesitant to incorporate museum collections into his class, a one-page "Suggestions for Museum Instructors" could have prevented the misunderstanding. The suggestions sheet could be circulated to all instructors prior to classes and could outline guidelines, suggestions, and procedures for presenting effective adult programs in the museum setting. Such guidelines represent a low-cost, time-saving way of disseminating information. A sample suggestion sheet is included in appendix A.

## Instructor Evaluations

Much has been written on evaluation procedures, but mostly as they relate to program evaluation in formal settings. Judy Diamond's *Practical Evaluation Guide* offers excellent guidance on developing evaluations for informal learning situations, such as those found in museums.[13]

In general, little attention has been given to evaluating instructors in informal programs. The offhanded approach of "Keep them until they lose their audience" is inadequate for any institution serious about improving instruction in museum programs. The basic principle in planning instructor evaluations is to include instructors in setting the evaluation criteria.[14] Once the criteria have been determined, they should be clearly communicated to all involved.[15]

Evaluations should reveal if educators have:

- Shown concern about learners as human beings

- Challenged learners to move beyond current levels of knowledge or ability

- Pointed out what was important to learn

- Promoted discussion and learner interaction

- Spoken with expressiveness and variety in tone of voice

- Used examples to illustrate concepts or practices

- Praised learners during the learning activities

- Appreciated prior knowledge of learners and made use of it during the activities so participants learn from each other

- Helped learners critically reflect on how they learn (this is especially relevant to transformative learning)[16]

The following methods are useful for conducting insightful instructor evaluations:

- *Interview:* This widely used method is suited to an in-depth exploration of issues. If interview questions are open-ended, participants' unique responses can shed light on why the activities are viewed differently by diverse groups. Productive interviews take time and require trained interviewers.

- *Observation:* Both qualitative and quantitative data can be gathered through observation, either in person or by using a video recorder. Observers are usually given a short list of things to look for that may include the extent of participation and personal interaction, nonverbal indicators of interest or inattention, and leadership roles.

- *Group Discussion Assessment:* Everything from course expectations to facilities might be evaluated in a group discussion assessment. Discussions can take the form of focus groups created specifically for the evaluation and composed of a cross section of participants or can simply be brainstorming sessions with participants.

- *Peer Review Panels:* Panels are convened to allow instructors to evaluate one another's work. A positive climate of constructive criticism is crucial when using this approach.

- *Rating Scales and Checklists:* Scales and checklists can easily be administered and revised. However, they are not the best methods to use when measuring attitudes or consequences of performance.[17]

Instructors who are able to integrate museum materials with good teaching strategies can help learners dialogue, reflect upon new insights, and apply them to all areas of their lives. Museum programs become dynamic learning situations when learners leave classes with lifetime learning goals. Instructors who take the time to identify good androgogical techniques, remain current in their knowledge area, and act as self-reflective practitioners will lead sessions that are productive for both themselves and their participants. In the next chapter, we consider those participants.

## Notes

1. Our research team settled on "instructor" when deciding what to call those who teach and lead any type of adult museum program, including classes, field schools, workshops, outreach programs, credit classes, and teacher workshops. "Teacher" is too often associated with children or authoritarian approaches. "Facilitator" has been suggested, since adults are more in control of their own learning, and "instructional leader," "manager of learning," "trainer," "group leader," and "resource leader" have all been used.

2. Alan Knox, *Helping Adults Learn: A Guide to Planning, Implementing, and Conducting Programs* (San Francisco: Jossey-Bass, 1986).

3. Don Seaman and Robert Fellenz, *Effective Strategies for Teaching Adults* (Columbus, Ohio: Merrill, 1989), 159.

4. Rosemary Caffarella, *Planning Programs for Adult Learners* (San Francisco: Jossey-Bass, 1994), 160.

5. Knox, *Helping Adults Learn*, 53.

6. Stephen Brookfield, *Understanding and Facilitating Adult Learning* (San Francisco: Jossey-Bass, 1986), 124.

7. Brookfield, *Understanding and Facilitating Adult Learning*, 124.

8. Seaman and Fellenz, *Effective Strategies*, 24.

9. Paulo Freire, *Pedagogy of the Oppressed* (New York: Herder and Herder, 1970).

10. Malcolm Knowles, *The Adult Learner: A Neglected Species* (Houston: Gulf, 1973), 223.

11. Seaman and Fellenz, *Effective Strategies*.

12. Knowles, *Adult Learner*, 223.

13. Judy Diamond, *Practical Evaluation Guide* (Walnut Creek, Calif.: AltaMira, 1999).

14. Sue McCoy, "Docents in Art Museum Education," in *Museum Education: History, Theory, and Practice*, ed. N. Berry and S. Mayer (Reston, Va.: National Art Education Association, 1989), 145.

15. Robert Fellenz, Gary Conti, and Don Seaman, "Evaluate: Student, Staff, Program," in *Materials and Methods in Adult Education*, ed. C. Klevins (Los Angeles: Kleven), 342.

16. David Deshler, "Measurement and Appraisal of Program Success," in *Program Planning for the Training and Continuing Education of Adults*, ed. Peter S. Cookson, 313–18 (Malabar, Fla.: Krieger, 1998).

17. Deshler, "Measurement and Appraisal," 313–18.

# CHAPTER FIVE

# PROGRAM PARTICIPANTS SPEAK OUT

Why are all the fun classes designed for kids? I want to play with putty and fossils and go on field trips to swamps too!

—Program participant

K ids can't wait to get out of school and adults can't wait to get back to class. This is a generalization, of course, but our study showed that adults are eager to learn new skills and broaden their understanding of history, art, science, and other subjects. Museums are well positioned to fill adult education needs. The more that museums and program planners know about the pool of adults clamoring for classes, the more precisely they will be able to attract and serve this important demographic niche.

## Anatomy of a Program Participant

Most adults attending museum programs are forty-five or older. They are college educated and many have done postgraduate work. Their primary purpose in attending museum programs is to learn and grow. And that they do. Program participants master skills that add to their enjoyment of life. They expand their relationships through interaction with others of similar interests. Some develop new attitudes and perspectives and gain new meaning in their lives. Some may even experience life-changing transformation.

*A Brief Demographic Overview of Adult Museum Program Participants*

- Thirty-two percent of adult museum participants are between the ages of forty and forty-nine.

- The highest correlation between age and increased program participation is among those ages fifty to fifty-nine.

- Program participation decreases for adults over sixty years of age, with a further decline beyond age seventy.

- Participants over sixty form a group equivalent in size to the under forty group (10 to 20 percent of program participants).

- The majority of program participants have a college degree, plus some postgraduate experience. There is a marked difference in the education levels of participants and the general population.

- More women than men participate in adult education programs,[1] though male and female participants were quite similar in age, education, motivation, and learning style, preferences, and outcomes.

- The high education level of most program participants suggests affluence. Fewer than 1 percent of survey respondents indicated that cost was a factor in deciding whether or not to attend a museum program.

**Table 5.1.   Relationship between Age and Program Participation**

| Age Groups | General Population | Program Participants | Participants/ Population |
|---|---|---|---|
| 18–29 | 22% | 10% | 0.45 |
| 30–39 | 21% | 12% | 0.57 |
| 40–49 | 21% | 32% | 1.52 |
| 50–59 | 14% | 25% | 1.79 |
| 60–69 | 10% | 13% | 1.30 |
| 70+ | 12% | 8% | 0.67 |

Source: A National Study of Adult Museum Programs, Bonnie Sachatello-Sawyer and Robert Fellenz, principal investigators, 1999.

## Adult Preferences: What Program Participants Want

Our research team asked 162 museum program participants to fill out a checklist that began with the question, "When participating in adult museum programs, how important for your learning and enjoyment is each of the following?" Respondents rated twenty program characteristics on a scale of one to five, with one being "not important" and five being "very important." Participants overwhelmingly felt that most of the factors presented rated a three (somewhat important), four (important), or five (very important).

**Table 5.2.    Important Aspects of Museum Programs as Rated by 162 Survey Participants**

When participating in adult museum programs, how important for your learning and enjoyment is each of the following?

|  | Very Important | Important |
|---|---|---|
| 1. Challenging content | 94% | 99% |
| 2. Dynamic, organized instructor | 92% | 99% |
| 3. Time for questions and discussion | 85% | 98% |
| 4. Learning how to get more info | 82% | 96% |
| 5. Getting close; having access | 80% | 94% |
| 6. Coming away with questions, ideas | 79% | 96% |
| 7. Feeling confident | 75% | 94% |
| 8. Having a pleasant experience | 74% | 95% |
| 9. Active, hands-on activities | 70% | 86% |
| 10. Talk to someone about topic | 70% | 95% |
| 11. Beginning with an overview | 68% | 91% |
| 12. Getting help to remember | 67% | 90% |
| 13. Interpretation of facts presented | 66% | 93% |
| 14. Comfortable physical setting | 64% | 89% |
| 15. Check out accuracy of ideas | 56% | 88% |
| 16. Interacting with other participants | 49% | 80% |
| 17. Connected to museum's purpose | 41% | 68% |
| 18. Attending with others you know | 29% | 49% |
| 19. Preparing beforehand | 23% | 57% |
| 20. Professionally dressed instructor | 16% | 39% |

As the checklist makes clear, program participants want challenging content, prefer dynamic and well-organized instructors, and expect access to objects and people not normally available to them. Adults want to participate in discussions and have the opportunity to talk with an expert. It is also very important for adult learners to feel confident about their ability to learn.

The aggregation of mid- to upper-range answers indicates that the success of museum programs is found in the sum of its parts. The exceptional experience is, in essence, the complete package. There were some notable exceptions, however. One-third of those surveyed indicated it was not important to have a program connected to the museum's purpose. Nearly half thought it was not personally important to prepare before attending a program. A little over half felt it wasn't important to attend with friends or family.

Responses to open-ended questions relating to content; instructors; questions and answers; access to objects, creatures, people, and places; hands-on activities; a comfortable setting; and interaction are described in more detail below.

## How Important Is New or Challenging Content?

*"I saw an ad in the paper that said something like 'Do you want to learn 230 pieces of new information?'"*

Docent, natural history museum

Most adult participants are highly educated. They want invigorating educational experiences at a museum, rather than simple entertainment.

## How Important Is a Dynamic, Well-Organized Instructor?

*"The most interesting part of the series was the way the instructor drew correlations between ancient Egyptian cultures and Native American and Christian cultures. I liked the way the instructor blended anecdotal and factual information."*

Program participant, natural history museum

The "perfect instructor" is organized, knowledgeable, dynamic, funny, flexible, communicative, caring, enthusiastic, efficient, willing to answer questions, tireless, famous, attractive, well dressed, and witty. (If you meet this person, hire him or her on the spot.) Great instructors are both entertaining and educational, with the entertainment factor effusing directly from personality and teaching ability, not from a canned attempt to amuse. Many program participants resonated with the instructor's use of anecdote to supplement teaching. Anecdotes and storytelling serve to humanize presentations and offer a break from the standard, didactic presentation. (Chapter 4 is devoted entirely to an examination of program instructors.)

### How Important Is Time for Questions and Discussion?

*"I especially enjoyed the interaction between members of the panel and between the panelists and the audience. The question-and-answer period was important."*

Program participant, history museum

For a strong majority of respondents, interaction was of the utmost importance and significantly contributed to an outstanding experience. Interaction with the instructor, with other program participants, or with both was regularly cited as what program participants remembered best or liked most about the program. We found no significant relationship between desire for interaction and age or gender.

Several program participants expressed displeasure with a program because of the lack of interaction. These comments show that interaction between presenters and participants is important in lecture settings as well as small-group discussions.

*"The class members weren't involved. There was no dialogue between the instructor and the class. The instructor just kept talking and talking with no breaks or opportunities for people to ask questions. There were no pauses in the presentation."*

Program participant, science museum

### How Important Is Getting Close to Objects, Creatures, People, or Places You Could Not Get Close to Otherwise?

*"I like having the opportunity to get into places I normally can't, like certain buildings or a private cave."*

Program participant, science museum

More than 80 percent of those surveyed listed the opportunity to get close to unique people, places, or objects as a motivation for attending museum programs. Museums are in the enviable position of being able to offer valuable learning opportunities by facilitating such access.

Adults want to see and experience authentic items, not replicas. At the Seattle Asian Art Center's saki tasting class, museum instructors used porcelain pieces from the collections to serve saki. Participants felt special handling the seventeenth-century Korean teacup that regular visitors might not even see, much less touch.

Access need not be limited to collections. Museums are perceived not only as repositories, but as keys to locked doors. Museum programs that take participants to a private cave, a rural commune, or a field station in Costa Rica all provide experiences not normally available to the public. Sights, smells, and sounds combine to create memorable experiences that may have a lasting and possibly transformative effect on participants. Field programs provide the most obvious opportunities for utilizing the environment as a learning tool. Participants at a program on maple sugaring repeatedly remarked on the beauty of the area and the falling snow as they learned about making maple syrup and maple sugar. Bird watching trips, afternoon hikes, camp outs, canoe adventures, and foreign travel programs all take advantage of new and interesting landscapes.

---

## CASE STUDY 5.1

### Native Uses of Plants: An Ethnobotany Class Offered at a Museum of Natural History

### Course Description

In this class, participants learned to identify edible and medicinal plants used by native peoples over the centuries. Wildcrafting principles, harvesting techniques, native legends, and recipes using wild foods were also covered. A lecture was presented on a Thursday night from 7:00 p.m. to 9:00 p.m. and a field trip was held on the following Saturday from 10:00 a.m. to 11:00 a.m. Cost was $35 for members, $45 for nonmembers.

### Institutional Perspective

Our mission to be the environmental science education center for the region and educate people about the natural world drives our approach to programming. Many of our courses focus on topics related to bioregional sustainability. Serving our membership is also important. The exhibits, especially new ones, also lead to some programs. I like to use the same format for every program. Programs usually begin with an evening lecture, which is followed by a field trip the next day. This lecture creates a better learning environment for the field trip because it provides participants with background information.

*continued*

I look for personable instructors who are experts in their fields, and contract with the museum's science staff for at least 80 percent of the hires. The instructor must be people oriented and have an engaging style of presentation. Instructors must also be flexible. If a program is not going well or if something unforeseen happens, the instructor has to adapt. The success of a class boils down to the success of the instructor.

Programs must break even financially. All programs must be on a solid financial foundation, but fulfilling our mission is more important than making money. Also, publicity is important, and I hope to hire a marketing expert for the education department, separate from the museum's public relations department.

I want our programs to be educational, fun, specialized, and unique—programs that can't be found anywhere else. I hope to see people learning about the natural environment and bonding with nature.

## Instructor's Perspective

I teach at a local community college and just recently began offering classes at the museum. Teaching at the community college is very different from teaching at the museum, because community college students are interested in a more general or self-help level of education. Museum program participants are more scholarly.

I have a great love for plants and am irresistibly drawn to the medicinal and spiritual aspects of Native American uses of plants. I feel Native Americans have a sort of reverence for plants that has been lost in our culture. My forte is inspiring the love of plants and their protection.

In my courses, I teach from an ethnobotanical point of view, giving background on the historical uses of the plants as well as presenting modern-day uses. I decide how to teach each class when I see who my audience is. At the beginning of the class, I ask participants what their special interests are and try to tailor the class to participants' needs. The legend and lore of plants is fascinating and I include them in my lectures. People tend to lose facts but will remember stories because they are more personal.

I used to have slides of plants, but now I try to bring in the plants themselves—one specimen of each plant I talk about in the class, including seeds, roots, and flowers if at all possible. I believe the feel of the plants helps people remember. I reinforce this with an herb walk so participants can see the living plants in their natural habitats.

The museum doesn't have any evaluation forms, so I bring my own forms to get feedback. Usually, a docent will sit in on one of my classes, or one of the participants who knows the education director will report back to her.

*continued*

**CASE STUDY 5.1 (continued)**

**PARTICIPANTS' PERSPECTIVES**

1. Connie
Education: some college
Age: thirty-seven
Occupation: owner of a small herb company

I took this class to learn more about the uses of native plants. I've signed up for several other classes at the museum (for both myself and my kids) that were canceled because of low enrollment. I think that's because the classes are only advertised to members.

This class helped me gain a greater appreciation of the native culture and I've been able to apply a couple of things I learned. For example, I learned that elderberry leaves can be used to make an insecticide spray, which I've made and used.

The only thing I didn't like about the program was the setting for the lecture on the first night. The seminar next door was often loud and disruptive. But all in all, the content and presentation were fine.

2. Madeline
Education: postgraduate degree
Age: sixty
Occupation: retired tour guide

I've been a member of the museum for twenty-four years and have taken several classes. In this one, I wanted to learn about the native uses of plants and to gain new and advanced ideas on the subject. I generally prefer lectures and, in particular, small seminars where people can interact better.

The presenter was excellent. She knew the subject thoroughly and presented it well. The class awakened something in me and stimulated an interest, and now I want to pursue the subject further.

**Research Observer's Perspective**

In the beginning and wrap-up of the lecture, the instructor talked about her belief in the sacredness of all life and her desire to protect and preserve native plants. I found her presentation very moving and it was nice to hear the instructor share something personal. Despite the description, the class seemed to focus more on the New Age medicinal values of plants than on traditional Native American uses.

The middle of the lecture seemed to drag. The instructor handed out a long list of plants and went down the list in an encyclopedic fashion: "manzanita, good for . . . , make a tea out of it. . . . yerba linda good for . . . , make an infusion out of it. . . ." The instructor brought in many plants from her own collection, but she just pointed to them at the front of the room.

*continued*

The lecture could have been dramatically improved by passing the plants around the room so everyone could examine them and reducing the number of plants listed. Since much of the lecture was devoted to the medicinal uses and preparations of specific plants (tea, infusion, poultice, and so on), the class might have benefited from some demonstrations. That would also have allowed the class to taste or otherwise experience the end products.

The second day was a whole different ball game. The instructor was obviously now in her element and the field trip was excellent. She encouraged a multisensory approach to examining plants, which was exceptional. Course participants listened to, looked at, touched, smelled, and ate plants found along the trail. One of the high points on the walking tour occurred when the instructor found a flowering plant that is fairly rare. She got very excited about seeing it and her excitement was contagious. There was little involvement during the lecture portion, but everyone was involved during the field trip. Course participants were very interested, asking questions and clearly enjoying the presentation. Also, the setting for the tour was exceptionally beautiful.

## Analysis

Although the museum has a stated preference for using the same format for every program (lecture plus field trip), a more social, interactive, experiential program in the classroom might have complemented the field experience better than a straightforward lecture. We have seen that instructors must be flexible, and that applies to the institution as well. A standard format for classes and field trips may work well most of the time, but it may be a barrier for some classes or some instructors.

The multisensory aspects of the field trip were outstanding. Tasting flowers in the wild is an excellent way to create a memorable experience. Likewise, smelling and touching leaves and flowers pulls people away from the usual looking and listening of most programs. We agree with the research observer that this multisensory learning could have been better incorporated into the classroom for this program. The program would have been much stronger if the instructor had enlisted the participants' help in cutting and grinding leaves, brewing tea, making poultices, and tasting or otherwise experiencing the results.

Program participants, however, did not express any dissatisfaction with the lecture portion of the field trip, with the exception of a complaint about ambient noise. The research observer seemed to be biased toward field programs versus lectures. Program participants felt the lecture portion of the program was just fine and were very positive about the overall experience. One program participant raved about the instructor as both knowledgeable and an excellent presenter. Once again, we see that the instructor's enthusiasm, expertise, and teaching ability are of the utmost importance in the success of a program.

## How Important Are Active, Hands-On Activities?

*"Museums should have more hands-on, real learning. I want to touch the old bones and use the old tools."*

Program participant, art museum

Over 70 percent of the adult program participants we surveyed indicated that they wanted hands-on activities. However, when asked about what they liked about a specific program, very few participants said they most liked the hands-on aspects of the program. Even in classes that were devoted to hands-on learning, like how to plant a wildflower garden or create a personal Web page, the instructor remained the primary positive aspect of the program.

Programs using an active, multisensory approach to learning are very popular. In a program on medicinal uses of native plants (see case study 5.1), program participants were encouraged not only to observe closely and touch a flower, but also to smell the fragrance and even taste the petals. The powerful taste of wild garlic flowers and the overall multisensory approach was indeed memorable and contributed significantly to the success of this program.

*Looking at butterfly eggs during a "bug walk" at the Chula Vista Nature Center.* (Courtesy Chula Vista Nature Center.)

## How Important Is a Comfortable Setting?

*"The chairs could have been more comfortable. Metal folding chairs are not very good for watching movies, and the sound system was poor."*

Program participant, art museum

Researchers logged numerous complaints about facilities: the chairs were uncomfortable, the room was too small, the room was too big, the room smelled bad, the parking garage smelled bad, the conditions were too rustic, the group next door was too loud, it was raining. Yet, when asked to rank the importance of comfort in a museum program, respondents attached less importance to this factor than we had anticipated. Our open-ended interviews did, however, show that a noticeably uncomfortable physical setting dramatically reduced the level of satisfaction for the program. Adults expect a program setting to be adequately comfortable. Program directors and instructors might consider using gallery halls or other collection areas, especially for small-group activities.

## How Important Is Interaction with Other Participants?

*"I had just retired and was vegetating. So I resolved to become involved in a learning activity. I missed the interaction with people so much."*

Docent, natural history museum

Making new friends was regularly mentioned as a long-lasting benefit from a museum program. It's important to note, however, that while most adults want time to interact with each other, others do not have any interest in participation or interaction. In fact, some program participants find interaction with other participants detrimental to their learning and enjoyment.

## What Participants Learned

Assessing outcomes of informal learning activities is a difficult process. In spite of this, our research staff believed it was important to find some new tools and offer estimates of what participants learned. In this study we collected information about learning by asking interviewees what they remembered about the program or how the program had changed them.

First we must note that participants' responses imply that a great deal of learning was occurring. Only two or three out of more than three hundred participants complained that they had learned little or nothing. The rest

*Trough making at the Red Butte Garden, Salt Lake City, Utah.* (Courtesy Red Butte Garden.)

talked enthusiastically about aspects of what they learned. In many cases, their learning went well beyond simple additive knowledge typical of adult learning to "big picture" concepts such as the notion that "scientific thinking and questioning is influenced by culture or what people are interested in."

Some of the adult learners had experiences they will remember forever, such as "actually sticking my hands in the dirt and finding a hadrosaur" or "the feeling of camaraderie." Others will remember "making connections between the music, literature, and art of a certain time period" or "learning about artists as people with lives and interests instead of just as names." Memories from such experiences are treasured and add spice to life. Museum programs are excellent sources for developing such special memories.

The interesting and informative answers to our questions on what participants remembered and how they were changed are summarized below according to the categories in our pyramid of learning outcomes (see chapter 1).

### Knowledge and Skill Mastery

The type of learning most frequently mentioned related to content knowledge. Nearly half of those queried specifically mentioned factual information. In general, these comments were also more global and connoted higher levels of cognitive knowledge, such as analysis or synthesis.

*I now have a mental picture of the various organs in my mind, so that when I read about a certain organ I know which one it is.*

Participant, organ tour

*The paleontological process is like collecting evidence at a crime scene. That's something I am very familiar with as a retired policeman. I see the measuring, photographing, and documentation as very similar to what I did in law enforcement, so I can relate the whole process to my personal experience.*

Participant, paleontology field school

*I will remember learning that scientific thinking and questioning is influenced by culture or what people are interested in.*

Participant, history of science lecture series

Acknowledgment of applying knowledge or skills came from people enrolled in skill classes. Apparently some of these incidences were the result of short, intensive experiences.

*I will definitely remember the "passage" technique that the docent spoke to us about. I had never heard of that technique before. I will also remember how she engaged the audience in telling her what we saw and how in such a short time (fifteen minutes) I learned so much about two pieces of artwork and a painter.*

Participant, spotlight tour

Two comments from people attending the same class point out similar skills that were developed, but different attitudes about their learning.

*I will remember the instructor's suggestions for buying saws, knife selection and sharpening techniques, how to peel a log for starting a one-match fire, digging fire pits for no-trace camping fires, using small fires for cooking, working with knots and ropes, mechanical advantages, pitching tents and lighting fires quickly, selecting rain gear and clothing for camping, and dealing with bears.*

Participant, wilderness skills class

*I will remember four knots and how to build one-match fires. I'll also remember that I liked the people in the class because they were intelligent, interesting, and interested in the topic.*

Participant, wilderness skills class

### Expanded Relationships

Participants frequently mentioned interaction with others as a major memory of museum experiences. As one particularly insightful program participant observed, "I think, because of the way our species is, that we tend to recall social interactions most vividly. Because this program is essentially a social activity in which learning takes place, I think the social interaction provides the context in which we recall the actual educational experience."

Her insight was supported by the comments of others. For example, "I remember the experience involved with learning with others who are just as interested and excited about the subject." Poignantly, another remembered "learning about sound from the deaf person in the class." Programs that provide opportunity for and encourage expanded relationships are both more effective and more enjoyable.

> *I will remember how the instructors challenged the participants to think and discover things on our own. They also challenged us to think about our feelings. I'll also remember sharing opinions and emotions with other participants.*
>
> Participant, docent training

Many others spoke of their learning in terms of instructors and instructors' techniques. Several insisted that it is the relationship of the teacher to the learner, rather than simply the words presented, that lead to learning. Teaching is an art appreciated by adult learners.

### Increased Appreciation or Meaningfulness

Lisa Roberts writes of learning in museums in terms of entertainment, empowerment, experience, and ethics, referring "to museum practices and visitor experiences that fall outside such traditional education goals as cognitive engagement and information transfer."[2] Roberts rejects the traditional view that such activities have no more redeeming outcome than pure and simple amusement. She insists that "older models of education based on hierarchical, unidirectional modes of communication no longer adequately describe the learning that occurs when visitors encounter objects. Education is not just about museums teaching visitors; it is about visitors using museums in ways that are personally significant to them."[3] Adults use their "free time," their recreation or vacation time, to attend museum programs. This supports the contention that they seek an entertaining learning environment. The entertainment we engage in influences the type of person we become.

The following statements support the notion that entertainment does result in learning by adult museum-goers.

*First and foremost I remember the enjoyable interaction with the other docents.*

*I will remember most the camaraderie of the docents.*

*I'll remember being impressed by the amount of sharing of information and ideas between instructors and docents and also remember everyone trying to help everyone else.*

*I remember the experience involved with learning with others who are just as interested and excited about the subject.*

Examples from sources as diverse as quantum physics and business practices seem to imply that our appreciation of the world around us depends greatly on our background. Roberts put it this way: "What we know, in other words, is based less on the nature of the object than on the manner and the context in which it is experienced."[4] This certainly confirms the idea that often the educational outcome of museum programs consists of new "meaning," not simply new "knowledge."

*I am much more curious about Lewis and Clark now. I want to do an even longer trip next summer. I am planning a trip with my family for next summer. It was an enlightening experience. I've done quite a bit of reading about the river, and about Lewis and Clark.*

Participant, Lewis and Clark canoe trip

Experiences have assumed a new role in today's society. According to Joseph Pine and James Gilmore, "Experiences are a new, distinct economic offering, as distinct from services as services are from goods, but one that until now went largely unrecognized." Businesses from restaurants to service groups are turning their offerings into "experiences" in which a customer "pays to spend time enjoying a series of memorable events that a company stages—as in a theatrical plan—to engage in a personal way."[5] Memories of museum participants support the notion that well-conducted museum programs can add appreciation and meaning to life.

*I've developed just a wonderful awareness of how things today interact with things of the past and a heightened awareness of the environment around me. The docent experience has gotten me excited again about learning and rekindled my curiosity about many things. As I go places, I look at things differently. When you take a trip, even though you may have been there a hundred times, you think differently.*

Docent, natural history museum

## Changed Attitudes or Emotions

Our staff was impressed by the large number of museum learners who spoke more of attitudes developed than of content learned. Comments concerning attitudes came from those attending a broad array of classes, from skill development programs and docent training, to a Plains Indian seminar and a gay/lesbian film series.

> *I will remember how the instructors challenged the participants to think and discover things on our own. They also challenged us to think about our feelings. I'll also remember sharing opinions and emotions with other participants. The program gave me a new perspective on art.*

Participant, docent training

> *This was a friendly, warm, fun, and humorous class, yet I could still ask specific, deep questions. I already knew about sequencing, DNA, fingerprinting, chemical processes, use of electricity, etc.*

Participant, popular genetics class

Warm, friendly, but challenging! The comments above are indicative of the feelings and emotions of many adults. The self-concepts of adults may not be as fragile as those of youth, but they can easily be threatened in learning situations. We all learn better in supportive situations where we don't have to defend ourselves while trying to analyze significant topics or tackle complex skills. Perhaps that is why so many adults used the word "fun" when telling us about learning situations they liked.

> *I remember being impressed with the instructor. He imparted his knowledge of how to arrange flowers, but more importantly, he gave me the confidence to make arrangements that are my own creation.*

> *I'll remember learning that it is not so important that flowers look perfect. I learned to let my creativity flow because no one was judging me. I was encouraged to attempt new techniques.*

Participants, flower-arranging class

Historically, there has been a tendency to avoid challenging participants on emotional and ethical issues in all types of adult education programs. Program managers have cautioned against potentially treading on value systems of the diverse audiences they are trying to attract. But in doing so, we neglect an essential component of human life and learning. Adult education professors Ralph Brockett and Roger Hiemstra agree that "ethics can be an emotionally charged topic and, as such, is often avoided. However, choosing not to address ethical issues can be very costly in terms of personal and institutional reputation, program effectiveness, and long-term success."[6] Also, museum mission statements often address ethical concerns related to environmental and cultural issues. Many programmers view controversial community issues involving ethical considerations as prime topics for adult sessions.

> *I'll remember the outstanding acting and the way the audience participated in the show. I remember the way I felt emotionally during the show. It really made me think twice about my view on the Human Genome Project and on science in general.*
>
> Participant, theater performance

Museum participants occasionally commented on learning related to attitude or belief systems. The comments below indicate adults considered ethical development an appropriate topic for museum programs.

> *I remember developing a world understanding of things. I gained a global and historical perspective on the world.... I remember learning about how the pressures and attitudes of people are important for understanding how people look at things and how science developed. I remember thinking about how this new perspective on history and science is important to our role in how the world is changing.*
>
> Participant, history of science lecture series

## Transformed Perspectives

Learning that transforms previously formed perspectives is learning primarily for adults. Its importance lies in the fact that, if we have not reflected in depth on perspectives formed earlier in life, we are bound to be limited to numerous contradictory, inadequate, or prejudicial elements within our perspectives. Bringing our perspectives up to date demands a healthy self-concept and a supportive atmosphere, plus an individual's critical acceptance that one's social relationships and culture have shaped his or her beliefs and feelings. As one docent said, "Learning seems to occur when museums help people to reflect on their own lives." Many museum programs do provide such support, as numerous program participants commented on change in their perspectives.

> *The class was fun. I will remember making connections between the music, literature, and art of a certain time period. I'll remember learning about artists as people with lives and interests instead of as just names.... I remember how*

*the people's emotional responses varied, even though they were all looking at the same art.*

Participant, art museum class

*I will remember the different perspectives of each speaker. One speaker in particular really piqued my interest and has made me want to read more on the subject because of the way he broadened the topic by incorporating it into a world perspective.*

Participant, local historic village symposium

Historically, there has been a tendency to "stay with science" and avoid interpersonal or ethical issues not just in museum programs, but in all types of adult education programs. Program managers fear treading on the value or belief systems of the diverse audiences they are trying to attract. However, museum participants did comment on learning related to value or belief systems that changed their perspectives. Adult learners often take holistic approaches to their learning and apply principles learned in one discipline to other aspects of life.

*I learned how the questions we ask determine the answers we get. There is so much interweaving of ideas and subjects. . . . I'll remember learning and realizing that people were, and are, looking at the world in different ways.*

Participant, history of science lecture series

*I remember the definition of chaos and will remember the basic concepts of the subject and how it applies to other things. I can relate chaos theory to problems with systems and working and communicating with people.*

Participant, mathematics lecture series

Informal learning implies that the participants have some control over the purpose of the learning session. This encourages or at least allows learners to broaden the application of principles and ideas to aspects of their lives and thus to applications well beyond the intentions of the instructor. This also encourages transformation of individuals' perspectives.

*I'll remember developing a world understanding of things. I gained a global and historical perspective on looking at the world. . . . I remember learning about how the pressures and attitudes of people are important for understanding how people look at things and how science developed. I also remember thinking about how this new perspective on history and science is important to our role in how the world is changing.*

Participant, history of science lecture series

*I also learned some things about the dynamics of museum work, especially that one cannot always be a perfectionist. It is OK to make a mistake as long as you learn from it. . . . I also learned how important communication is if you want to work together with a group.*

Participant, museum internship

## Life-Changing Experiences

*The docent program had a definite impact on me: I left physics. Astrophysics has taken a backstage to anthropology. The experience has opened an entirely new world for me. The program even changed how I spend my time. Before this I had never spent a second on life science.*

Docent, natural history museum

This vivid example of life-changing learning impressed our research staff. Willing to search the world for new insights, this learner was a highly respected tour leader and an inspiration to other docents. This example, of how a person dedicated to study and work in one area of science can change priorities and goals through learning in adulthood, demonstrates the potential power of museum programs.

It has been said that by the time we become adults we have had to put the world together in some order that makes sense to us. But we want to know more. As we grow intellectually, we recognize the gaps and errors in our image of life and reality. While it is fairly simple to broaden our knowledge, improve our skills, and adjust some insights, it is much more difficult to change basic assumptions and premises. These basic perspectives often result from past education and experiences and can be changed only through reflection on the presuppositions upon which they were based. This leads to adult learning in the strictest sense of the term, that is, learning possible only to a mature adult.

Museum programs seem ideal occasions for life-changing learning. Adults participate primarily to learn. Fellow participants are also eager learners with varied backgrounds and perspectives. Instructors not only possess a certain expertise but usually also hunger for further learning.

*I learned how the questions we ask determine the answers we get. There is so much interweaving of ideas and subjects. . . . I'll remember learning and realizing that people were and are looking at the world in different ways.*

Participant, history of science lecture series

*The field school had a profound effect on me. I am back in school and intend to pursue paleontology. The staff were very supportive of me and their behavior was the catalyst.*

Participant, field school

## Finding Direction

Most of the adults attending museum programs are forty-five years old or older and well educated. Their primary purpose in attending museum programs is to learn. Above all, they want challenging content and a dynamic instructor. As active learners, they want time for questions and answers and to know how to locate additional resources. In general, they want instructors who are knowledgeable and flexible, and with whom they can interact. Apparently, this pertains not just to "knowledge seekers" but also to "museum lovers," who take pride in quality programs, and "skill builders," who want excellent training. "Socializers" are engaged by challenging content, which stimulates interaction with others. These motivational responses indicate that adults want invigorating educational experiences at a museum rather than simple entertainment.

When learning in museums, adults want better access to places, collections, and cutting-edge ideas. The unique experiences they gain through better access serves to broaden their experience base and invite new ideas and memories. As one art and music class participant said, "I will remember making connections between the music, literature, and art of a certain time period. I will remember learning about artists as people with lives and interests instead of as just names."

Experiences have clearly assumed a new role in today's society. They are an important economic offering, one that museums should capitalize on. Businesses such as restaurants and service-oriented enterprises are turning their offerings into "experiences" in which a customer "pays to spend time enjoying a series of memorable events that a company stages—as in a theatrical plan—to engage in a personal way." The challenge for museums is to find new ways to use their assets to create motivational, life-changing experiences that continue to influence adults' future decisions about learning long after the programs end. Some suggestions on how to get started are offered in chapter 6.

# Notes

1. National Center for Education Statistics, *Adult Education Survey* (Washington, D.C.: National Center for Education Statistics, 1998).

2. Lisa C. Roberts, *From Knowledge to Narrative: Educators and the Changing Museum* (Washington, D.C.: Smithsonian Institution Press, 1997), 131.

3. Roberts, *From Knowledge to Narrative*, 132.

4. Roberts, *From Knowledge to Narrative*, 132.

5. Joseph Pine and James Gilmore, "The Experienced Economy," *Museum News* 78, no. 2 (1999): 45.

6. Ralph G. Brockett and Roger Hiemstra, "Philosophical and Ethical Considerations," in *Program Planning for the Training and Continuing Education of Adults*, ed. Peter S. Cookson (Malabar, Fla.: Krieger, 1998), 131.

# CHAPTER SIX

# DESIGNING EXCELLENT LEARNING EXPERIENCES

Designing educational programs is a practical art.
> —Rosemary Caffarella, adult education researcher

Successful adult museum programs foster learning, build friendships, fuel membership, provide political support, promote a positive image for the museum, and more often than not pay for themselves. A good program is challenging and informative, piques curiosity, and stimulates critical thinking. An *excellent* program can change people's lives by opening the door to new ways of thinking, seeing, and ultimately, being. What can program planners do to create this sort of meaning-making experience? The answer is as simple as it is complex: facilitate critical self-reflection in instructors and program participants.[1]

Program planners can structure opportunities for such reflection by consciously designing programs that specifically serve the needs of adult learners. Remember that critical reflection and discourse are not limited to the learning experience, but can also be used by planners throughout all stages of the program-planning process, from brainstorming to program planning, announcement, marketing, delivery, and evaluation.

## R.E.A.L. Experiences

As a result of our involvement in this study, the way we think about and create adult programs has changed. Each team member has had his or her own transformative experience along the way. Consequently, in 2000 several of us jotted down our own core values for programs and described the methodology for creating what we have come to call "R.E.A.L. experiences" (Realizing Excellence in Adult Learning). Not surprisingly, individual learners are at the center of the R.E.A.L. experience. We offer these steps as tools for creating, improving, or rethinking your total package of programs for adults and empowering your communities as a result. Many of these steps can be done simultaneously. We also offer this approach as a first step toward encouraging the museum field at large to think about planning and evaluating programs using the impact on an individual, instead of numbers served, as a starting point. Think about measuring change in individuals' lives. Can we measure how others appreciate an idea? Can we change attitudes? Can we transform perspectives? Can we change people's lives? There will be times when people will walk in your door, then walk back out forever changed in powerful, transformative ways. Experiment, take some risks, come up with some new crazy ideas and *never doubt you have extraordinary personal power to change people's lives through excellent museum programs.*

## Step One: Create the Vision—Create Excellence

First and foremost, successful programs begin with a vision shared by all those involved in the planning process. Before planning any actual programs, plan a retreat away from the museum with staff and other immediate stakeholders. Answer the following questions to help focus and guide your overall program plan:

- What are your core values (guiding principles) as a person?
- What core values do you share with your staff and instructors?
- What does your museum do that no other institution can do?
- What kinds of experiences do you want adults to have at your museum?
- When people talk about your museum, what do they say?
- Why does your institution exist?
- Who cares about what you do?
- What is your vision for your educational programs?
- How will you "brand" your adult education programs?

After you've answered these questions, write the answers down and articulate them every day in every creative way you can. Next, identify internal and external sources of support, in terms of both commitment and action. Commitment is expressed in written and verbal support from the administration and board. Action involves people at all levels and takes the shape of budget allocations, access to other resources, and actual involvement in the program.[2]

Internal sources or institutional support may include mission statements, vision statements, standard operating procedures, administration, curatorial, marketing, and program-planning staff, and financial resources. All staff should draft and share a common vision for excellent programs and exhibits.

External sources include individuals, agencies, and organizations outside the museum and take into account the community's social, economic, and political climate.[3] Commitment and action are important in collaborations with outside organizations and contract instructors. For example, a cooperating organization can highlight a successful museum program at an annual meeting or the museum director can acknowledge the important work of an organization with which the museum is collaborating.

Once the sources have been identified, invite key shareholders, including funding agencies, community and organizational leaders, potential program participants, and instructors to share in the actual program-planning process. People will be more supportive if they have been included from the beginning. Create a collaborative environment for the exchange of ideas and open dialogue.

---

The Fort Worth Museum of Science and History envisions "Extraordinary Learning Environments" for their programs:

FORT WORTH MUSEUM OF SCIENCE AND HISTORY'S
STONE TABLETS

DEFINITION OF AN EXTRAORDINARY LEARNING
ENVIRONMENT (ELE):
AN ELE IS A STIMULATING, MULTI-DIMENSIONAL, IMMERSIVE PLACE WHERE VISITORS HAVE OPPORTUNITIES TO HEAR REAL STORIES, INTERACT WITH COOL STUFF, CONSTRUCT THEIR OWN KNOWLEDGE AND BECAUSE OF THEIR EXPERIENCE, THE VISITOR WILL NEVER BE THE SAME.

*(continued)*

WHAT AN ELE SHOULD BE:
Fun
Immersive (for a while you forget everything else)
Encourage discovery
Learner driven
Stimulating
Multi-dimensional
Accessible
Resource efficient
Connected

VISITORS WILL HAVE THE OPPORTUNITY TO:
See and touch cool, real stuff
Hear stories
Test their ideas
Have fun
Catch yourself doing something you never thought
you would do
Do things you can not do at home or in school
Play
Interact with others
Experience A-HA!

WHAT HAPPENS TO THE VISITOR BECAUSE OF THEIR
EXPERIENCE:
SHORT TERM
Laugh
Eyes light up
Curious
Emotionally stimulated
Out of the ordinary experience
Gain confidence/competence cusp
LONG TERM
Gain confidence/competence cusp
Deeper relationship with their world
Develop perspective
Experience personal growth

## Step Two: Identify Audiences—Old Friends and New

### What Do Adults in Your Community Care About?

Before you can begin to plan effective adult educational programs, you need to know more about the adults in your community. What is important to them? Why? The best way to collect this information is often by engaging in dozens of one-on-one conversations. What do adults in your community care about? What is the age, gender, educational level, household income, race, or nationality of your target audience or audiences? What are their interests and hobbies? What do they do in their leisure time? What are their opinions on various community issues? What motivates them to attend museum programs? How often do they attend educational programs? What other resources are available in your museum? Has the marketing department conducted any visitor studies? What other adult leisure studies have been conducted by other entities (e.g., chamber of commerce) in your community? Armed with information about the clusters of adults in your community, you are in a better position to make decisions about the types of adult programs you will plan and offer.

The majority of participants in museum programs are self-selected; that is, they are already museum users and inclined to attend educational programs. Frequent adult museum visitors and program participants are generally well educated, relatively affluent, Caucasian, between the ages of forty and sixty, female, and have more leisure time than the average American adult. But what about the rest of the world? If the museum wants to serve individuals in the broader community, it has to seek them out and welcome them in. *Adults need just as much targeted attention as children do.*

> *The challenge of accommodating new audiences in adult and continuing education can appropriately be met by becoming familiar with the emerging groups, researching their foremost needs and concerns, and finding or creating culturally sensitive methods to meet those needs.*
>
> L. C. Valazquez, "New Market Audiences in Continuing Education"

Below are some ideas on drawing a more diverse clientele.

*Use Market Research to Identify Existing and Potential Audiences*

If you are serious about building your audience, consider investing in professional market research to identify potential audiences and their interests. One national arts marketing firm with whom our research team spoke uses dozens of market indexes to identify clusters of potential audiences in a community.[4] The firm can describe in detail what these adults do, what they value, and how they choose to spend their leisure time. They follow demographic analysis with in-depth interviews to get a better sense of the individuals who make up these clusters—who they are and under what circumstances they choose to participate in museum activities. Once you know who your target audiences are, you can make sure your programs meet their needs.

*Make It a Goal to Attract New Audiences*

Make it a goal to attract a certain percentage of participants from new audiences each programming year. Write down what new adult audiences you want to attract and what you already know about them. Find out more about how they like to spend their leisure time, when they have free time, with whom they spend it, and what they value. While developing new audience sectors, be sure to continue to provide excellent programs for your core audience.

## Step Three: Generate and Investigate Program Ideas

### Brainstorm

With a clear understanding of who your target groups are, list the types of programs they might be attracted to. Invite staff, current and potential participants, instructors, and community members to brainstorm together on what experiences you can create. A program planner from one institution meets regularly with teachers, volunteers, and tour operators and requests program ideas. Look for ways to match community needs with museum resources. For example, ask your volunteers:

What can we offer "knowledge seekers"?
What can we offer "museum lovers"?
What can we offer "socializers"?
What can we offer "skill builders"?
What are our assets as a museum?
How can we provide better access to people, places, and things?

### Gather Information

There are a variety of methods for gathering information and feedback on ideas generated in the brainstorming sessions. The method used will depend on your budget, time frame, and need for detailed information. Common information-gathering techniques include:

- Formal needs assessment

- Conversations with colleagues, friends, family, program participants, instructors, and acquaintances

- Program observations by independent evaluators

- Questionnaires and written surveys

- In-depth interviews with participants and nonparticipants

- Focus group sessions with participants and nonparticipants

- Reviews of comparative educational programs

- Prior program records and reports

While developing new audience sectors, be sure to continue to provide
excellent programs for your core audience.

## Step Four: Sort and Prioritize Program Ideas

Once program ideas have been identified and investigated, planners need
to sort and prioritize. Answering the following questions can help in judging a program's value.

### Consider the Four Essentials

Successful programs take into account four essential components:

- *Learner:* Adult learners are experienced, active, responsible, and enthusiastic.
- *Instructor:* The instructor's knowledge, interpersonal skills, and style of
  presentation can make or break a program.
- *Content:* Careful selection of program content can lead to new knowledge
  and skills and ultimately result in inspirational and life-changing experiences for participants.
- *Context:* In the best learning environments, adults feel both physically
  and psychologically safe, supported, and respected.

These four components are melded together through insightful program and
instructional design. A little tweaking of weaker components can turn an
"okay" program into a highly successful one.

Does this program:

- Advance the museum's mission?

- Help "brand" the learning experiences you want to deliver?

- Complement the museum's exhibits and collections?

- Have the potential to improve the quality of adult lives?

- Project a positive image for the museum?

- Involve collaboration with other organizations?

- Fit available resources (personnel, facilities, money, and equipment)?

Don't throw away ideas because they overreach your museum's capabilities or resources. Plan to develop related alternatives if the initial ideas are unrealistic. Collaboration with curators and other organizations may help bring more extensive programs into the realm of possibility. However, make sure you do not lose your own institution's identity in the process.

## Step Five: Develop Program Goals and Objectives

What is your overall goal for a particular program? To draw new audiences to the museum? To promote learning? To develop good community relations? To improve the quality of participants' lives? Program goals and objectives should be clearly written, communicated, and understood by all parties, including participants, instructors, and sponsoring agencies. Clear objectives help program planners select materials, outline content, select teaching methods, and prepare evaluation procedures.[5] Articulating objectives also ensures that class descriptions in brochures and catalogs are accurate and informative. Participants should be able to match their own objectives with those of the course.

## Step Six: Incorporate a Combination of Experiences

What combination of experiences will define your programs? A single-faceted program is like a plain tomato pizza. It may be enough for some appetites, but most adult learners appreciate a little complexity. The best programs for adults are "combos." Or, as business consultant Joseph Pine has said, they are "all-encompassing, with entertaining, educational, escapist, or aesthetic elements."[6] In our study, we found that excellent museum experiences generally incorporate some combination of the following:

- Knowledge acquisition (grasping new ideas, actively learning something new)

- Practical skill building (trying something new, learning a new skill)

- Physical challenges (physical activities or sports)

- Interpersonal interactions (sharing personal stories, discovering relationships)

- Intrapersonal interactions (self-reflection, emotion, readiness for change)

- Spiritual connections (connections with life, death, spirits, the paranormal)

- Aesthetic experience (immersion in art, music, or landscape)

- Outdoor adventure (immersion in a new or disorienting environment)

- Entertainment (fun activities, humorous instructor or participants)

## Step Seven: Determine Formats, Schedules, and Staffing Needs

Program format refers to the structure and organization of an educational activity (lecture, workshop, dramatic presentation). It is inherently linked to what you are trying to accomplish. For example, if your primary goal for adult programs is to have a positive impact on adult lives, consider developing more learner-centered, multisession workshops or field trips that reconnect participants with the museum over an extended period of time.

When program planners are ready to develop new kinds of programs, several factors need to be considered, such as: (1) What is the most appropriate format? (2) What are the optimum times of day and year to offer the program? (3) What staff are needed to deliver the program? When planners prepare to adjust existing programs, there are other factors to be considered. For example, what existing programs are so institutionalized that they are difficult to change? Are there instructors who have to be rehired for political or financial reasons? To get started . . .

- **Choose the Most Appropriate Format for the Learning Activity**
  The format used will depend on program goals and content, the target audience's experience and background, the instructor's teaching experience, the museum's mission, and the availability of facilities, equipment, materials, and other resources. Program formats can range from learner-centered approaches like mentoring or individual learning contracts to large-group or community learning formats such as conferences or lectures. By offering a variety of program formats, museums can reach a broader audience with a wider range of learning styles. Take a little risk and try offering more multipart outdoor discussions, field trips, or theater experiences. What really counts? (See chapter 2 for a more detailed examination of program formats.)

- **Create a Program Schedule That Is Compatible with the Participants' Personal Commitments**
  Between family, work, and school, adults have many commitments. The season or time of day a program is offered will often determine whether or not adults can attend. Duration is also a concern. Some participants prefer intensive workshops, while others like shorter classes spread out over a longer period of time.
  Of course, scheduling for the convenience of the majority may still not work for many individuals. Some museums offer popular programs with a choice of times to serve people with varying schedules and needs. For example, many older adults prefer not to drive after dark. A popular program offered in the afternoon as well as at night might satisfy both older participants and people with nontraditional work schedules.

- **Identify Dynamic Program Presenters**
  Create a job description for both internal and external program presenters and advertise new teaching opportunities. Consider re-

cruiting potential instructors from culturally, geographically, and economically diverse parts of the community. Observe programs by other organizations within the community. To find new instructors, attend community programs and follow up on recommendations from staff, board members, colleagues, peers, volunteers, community leaders, program participants, and other instructors. Keep in mind the qualities that make a good instructor. (See chapter 3 for the program planner's perspective on choosing instructors and chapter 4 for the instructor's perspective.) Create a formal contract with them so their responsibilities and yours are clearly defined (see appendix B for a sample contract).

## Step Eight: Consider the Instruction Strategy

Naturally, a program's format influences the choice of teaching strategy, although a great deal of instructional flexibility exists regardless of format.

The instructional strategy should be chosen as consciously as the program content. Interactive classes or discussion groups led in a casual and familiar way are appropriate for small groups. More formally delivered lectures or symposia may be most effective for larger groups. (Adding multimedia or a touch of drama to lectures makes this format more engaging for learners.) A straightforward presentation may work well for the dissemination of fact-based material, while discussions are more suitable for problem solving and interactive approaches are better for skill development. Using a combination of methods is often very effective.

Before planning program budgets, have a conversation with the museum director to find out whether adult programs will be subsidized by operating funds or are expected to break even, be self-supporting, or make a profit. Program planners may want to negotiate to keep all or part of the proceeds from registration fees to experiment with new programs or develop others that will not cover all of their expenses. Program planners will also need to know the amount of money that will be available for marketing programs and who will determine the priorities for those funds. Often the marketing department controls this budget, making interdepartmental cooperation and coordination essential to success. Time spent working with the marketing department to align your respective visions for adult programs is time well spent.

## Dialogue-Based Learning at the Getty

*Though many of the museum's teaching staff and docents are gaining comfort with dialogue-based learning, it is not easy. Most of us have never experienced such an approach in our own formal education, so we have few models on which to rely. For this reason, ongoing training in the effective use of dialogue-based teaching strategies is central to helping us develop and hone our skills for actively engaging the visitor in the learning process.*

Karen Giles, manager of Adult and
Community Programs, J. Paul Getty Museum

According to Giles, dialogue-based teaching is, at its best, an artful blend of three things:

- Providing a structure for looking
- Sharing pertinent and engaging information
- Listening to the learners' ideas and questions and weaving those into the learning experience

The Getty has been exploring the use of dialogue-based teaching strategies with adult audiences since the mid-1990s. The approach is used by all teaching staff, including paid gallery teachers who provide gallery talks and volunteer docents who lead architecture and garden tours. These talks and tours are characterized by a balanced juxtaposition of such elements as looking activities, information dissemination, writing or drawing activities, and open-ended questions that stimulate and facilitate discussion. This kind of experience enables visitors to gain confidence in looking at and responding to works of art on their own. In the course of forty-five minutes to an hour, groups examine four to five works of art, architectural features, or garden elements in depth, rather than many objects or elements in a cursory fashion.

The dialogue-based teaching approach helps visitors develop a structure for making sense of what they see. It encourages sharper perceptions and more nuanced interpretations and gives learners an opportunity to share perceptions and ideas and to consider connections between art and their own lives. By bringing the learners' voices into the learning process, the gallery teacher or docent can better respond to audience needs and interests. Basing a museum tour on dialogue creates an experience more akin to how adults learn in everyday life through observation, participation, and conversation.

## Step Nine: Prepare a Budget

### Evaluate Costs and Financing

Ideally, everyone involved in the planning process should have access to budget information.[7] To get started:

- Evaluate costs and funding.

- Estimate expenses, including costs for program development, delivery, and evaluation. Key budget elements to consider include staff and instructor salaries and benefits, instructional materials, facility costs, food, travel, equipment, promotional materials, external consultants, research, and miscellaneous associated costs.

- Determine how the program will be financed. Program planners and marketing staff should understand funding resources and be familiar with the administration of each revenue source. Possible sources of income include operating funds from the parent institution; participant fees; sales from materials, publications, or services; grants or contracts from private organizations, individuals, or foundations; federal, state, or local funding; and profits from past programs.[8]

- Compare income and expense estimates to determine where you stand.

In the end, some adult museum programs pay for themselves, others do not. If the overall goal of your adult programs is to improve the quality of program participants' lives, you will naturally develop some into "cash cows" that support other programs for the greater community good. Programs that do not pay for themselves, whether they are offered for fewer numbers of adults or at a reduced cost, are expected to be offered and are supported especially when it can be documented that they have had a significant impact on individuals.

### Pricing Strategies

Pricing decisions affect who can attend programs and will influence the public's interest in and perception of the program. This is true whether students pay for programs themselves, share the cost with others, or have fees paid entirely by third parties.[9]

Competition, demand, the total cost of planning and implementing the program, tradition, and previous practice affect the admission price of a program. At the same time, pricing structures should be appropriate to consumer needs and value perceptions, the life cycle of the program, and environmental conditions.[10] If a museum offers a program in an economically depressed neighborhood, the institution can consider deferred payment plans, differential pricing, discounting, or scholarships. If two similar programs are offered, one at a higher cost, make sure consumers know they are getting more for their money in the more expensive program. In a highly competitive market, lowering the cost will sometimes attract more participants.

Develop a diversity of programs with a wide range of fees and take into consideration travel costs for program participants. Create a pricing strategy that offers affordable programs for families and more expensive, exclusive experiences for adults-only groups. "No more than 49 percent of your activities should be priced within a 15 percent range," argues Julie Coates of the Learning Resource Network (LERN). "Diversity in price is important, not only from an income or financial point of view, but [also because it] allows your program to reach different markets that respond to different price levels."[11]

Consider scholarship opportunities, special incentives (such as course coupons), and other rewards for repeat program participants, volunteers, early registrants, and multiple registrants from the same organization.

## Step Ten: Get the Word Out—Marketing Museum Programs

Programs start the minute you announce them. Start creating experiences in adult minds by whetting their appetites in the advertising. Like in cooking, the spice is in the sauce. Spend time to create the right flavor by creating engaging, detailed descriptions and graphics, with a spike of fun.

You might have a dynamite program aimed at a specific audience, but without marketing it may never reach an audience, let alone its full potential. Marketing is the "overall design and management of a well-coordinated plan" to promote, sell, and distribute a product or service.[12] Effective marketing, advertising, and publicity strategies are an essential part of producing an excellent learning experience.

Program planners do well to develop a vision, a brand name, and a reputation for excellence. Successful program planners distinguish their programs from others in the community by knowing and articulating their museum's mission and vision for educational experiences. They "brand" their vision and use it consistently in all advertising, publicity, and communication.

## Branding: A Not-for-Profit Strategy

*by Stephen Brand, President and Chief Imagination Officer,*
*The New Enterprise Factory, Inc.*

Branding is an overused term at conferences and in the media, but what does it actually mean? Do museums, zoos, and other cultural organizations need to be "branded"? Branding is the conscious construction of an image. Some corporations are now using the phrase "corporate DNA" as a way to express the way in which core values and missions can be "branded" into all of a company's activities, materials, products, policies, and services.

In the not-for-profit world, branding your organization's mission and core values is the way you distinguish yourself from others. It's what makes the Bronx Zoo different from the San Diego Zoo or, for that matter, Sea World. It's image. What do you think about when you hear the name of a particular institution? How do you feel when you walk through their gates or their doors?

Branding can help a not-for-profit organization stay true to its mission and consistent in its message. A branding strategy can guide what your team says to guests, what your building looks like, how your print materials are designed—in short, how people feel when they enter your world. A strong image can also attract funders who clearly understand what your institution is all about and want to lend support.

One of my favorite branded companies is Southwest Airlines. When you call Southwest and get put on hold, you don't get the usual, "we'll get to you" message. You get someone singing a song about how horrible it is to wait on the phone. What is the Southwest Airlines brand? Fun, entertaining, customer friendly, experience driven. A company that understands—and tries to remedy—the frustrations of travel. Southwest Airlines filters everything it does to fit the Southwest brand.

Think of your favorite museums or attractions. What do they conjure up in your mind? Compare your image of the Experience Music Project in Seattle, Washington, to your image of the Henry Ford Museum in Dearborn, Michigan. An organization's branding might come through in:

- Marketing materials
- Program strategies
- Construction materials
- Policies for personnel, public interaction, and operations
- Internal communication and design of team (staff) meetings
- Speeches that the CEO makes in the community
- Signage around your building
- How you establish your budget priorities

*continued*

- Who you hire
- Chaperone policies
- Whether you have a presence at community events
- Who you establish partnerships with
- The clothing or uniform your team wears
- Signage in your bathrooms
- Exposed walls
- How you treat your live animals
- How you train your team
- What titles you have for your executives and other staff
- Whether you will close the building for a special event and keep out the general public
- And on and on

The key is to develop an effective branding program and then infuse everything you do with it. Train employees how to use the branding strategy in all actions and decision making. Explain the positive ways in which a strong branding effort can affect the organization. Being an organization with a brand doesn't mean that you are "Disneyfied." It just means that you are clear about who you are.

## What Can a Good Branding Effort Do for Your Organization?

- Help streamline decision making in expenditures, marketing, experience development, hiring, and many other areas
- Help employees effectively develop recommendations for change
- Help employees who are challenging your organizational culture to look for another job in a place that is more in line with their values and passions
- Help focus your marketing efforts
- Help create a filter for adding new experiences and getting rid of others
- Limit debates or at least provide a foundation for dialogue within your organization
- Help funders understand what you are about and who you are

## How Do You Develop This Branding Effort?

There are many ways to go. Some say you have to spend a lot of money for branding to work; some say it just takes attention to detail and listening to guests and employees.

- You can hire a consultant to evaluate your brand and recommend a strategy that will tie all of your public image elements together

*continued*

- You can start with a strategic planning effort, creating a solid mission, core values, and set of image filters
- You can pay attention to the details of your experience
- You can have different departments talk to each other and compare notes—a novel idea!

### Will You Have to Rebrand?

You must reevaluate your branding on a regular basis. Is it true to your mission? Does your audience, or any audience out there, support your brand or get inspired by your message? Is your branding consistent with your community mission? Does it distinguish you from everyone else?

Changes happen every day. Your brand may need to adapt to changing trends in demographics, cultural passions, societal norms, employee and leadership vision, and many other things.

Branding is not just a logo and new stationery—it is deep and pervasive and reaches into the hearts and minds of everyone involved and the roots of everything you do.

## Eleven Key Steps in Developing a Marketing Plan

- Articulate the overall mission and goals of the organization

- Analyze the product, consumer, marketplace, and competition

- Define advertising and marketing objectives

- Pinpoint the target audience

- Determine the budget

- Formulate the message strategy

- Select the optimal media mix

- Coordinate advertising with other elements within the promotional mix

- Execute the campaign

- Measure results

- Evaluate the effectiveness

## Get a Feel for the Marketing Environment

Programs are more likely to succeed when consideration is given to the marketing environment. Scrutinize the local service area for its demographic, economic, ecological, technological, political, and sociocultural climates.[13] Here are some questions to think about:

- How strong is the local economy? If unemployment is high, people may not be able to afford programs.

- Do local politicians support your institution and the services it provides? Elected officials can influence funding decisions for programs.

- Do your programs reflect the needs and preferences of various community members?

- What is the competition? If there are already too many similar programs within the local service area, you may have a difficult time drawing participants. Perhaps you may want to investigate possible collaborations.

Here program planners can be important change agents within an institution. They can proactively work to improve relationships with the people in the marketing department, thus learning more about their work and how to support it. At one museum, education and marketing staff arrange to have a monthly lunch at which they can talk informally about opportunities. Planners also invite marketing staff to attend programs free of charge.

## Do You Need Professional Help?

Some people make their living monitoring the marketing environment, anticipating trends, and determining the best ways in which to respond. Do you have the time or personnel to do so? If not, can you afford to bring in an outside marketing firm? If you decide to contract with an outside marketing consultant, be sure to address the following items before entering into an agreement:

- Exactly what do you want to know?

- What audience(s) are you targeting?

- Do you have the support of museum administration and other key departments?

- What are you going to do with this study?

- How does your study relate to institutional goals?

- How will you select a research firm?

- How much time do you have for your study?

- What is your budget?

- Can the study include professional development opportunities for staff?

- How will you bring your researcher "up to speed" on your institution?

- Who will be your on-site liaison with the researcher?

- How will the researcher assist you in understanding the results?

By studying your market, you will learn what the potential demand is for the types of programs you are offering. After completing several professional marketing analyses with ArtsMarket Inc., the Strong Museum in Rochester, New York, refocused its exhibits, museum services, and programs to serve the needs of young families with children. By effectively serving needs of young mothers and targeting them in marketing efforts, the museum increased membership by more than 300 percent and attendance by more than 100 percent over a four-year period.[14]

## Match the Right Marketing Strategies to Your Target Audiences

Explore how your target groups find out what's happening in the community. Do they regularly read the paper, watch public television, listen to public radio, read church bulletins? Adults with a high level of education tend to look to media and experts as sources of information, while adults with less formal education (approximately two-thirds to three-fourths of the public) tend to rely mainly on conversations with family and friends.[15] In some communities word of mouth may reach a broad audience, in others it does not.

Our study found that adults who participated in museum programs obtained information from the Internet, newspapers, magazines, public television, National Public Radio, local colleges, and libraries. If they were connected to the Internet (58 percent were when this study was conducted, from 1996 to 1999), they used it several times a week to obtain information. Many museums like the California Academy of Sciences list their courses on-line and offer on-line access to course outlines and other resources for participants.

---

**Spreading the Word**

Here are a few tips for spreading the word about programs:

- Provide feeder classes in a more convenient and comfortable location as a way to entice people into the main program.
- Publicize a human-interest story about someone who has had an inspirational, fun, or life-changing experience in a program at your museum.
- Identify the target audience's opinion leaders (individuals to whom people look for information and attitudes). These opinion leaders can be, for example, bartenders, feed-store operators, or newspaper columnists. Learn how they view your institution. Find ways they can help you get the word out on educational opportunities.

*Source:* Alan Knox, "Adults as Learners, *Museum News* 59, no. 5 (1981): 24–29.

---

Other museums are starting to use bar-coding systems to track members' use of the museum. They then follow up with a targeted e-mail or letter offering more programs and museum services similar to the ones they participated in. At one museum, the membership department sends out weekly e-mail messages to members featuring weekly program offerings and updates on ticket availability. With up-to-date participant profiles (see appendix F) in a computer database, program planners could also send targeted e-mail messages about classes and workshops to those most likely to participate.

### Advertising

Class bulletins, program brochures, and institutional catalogues are commonly used to promote educational programs, but this is not necessarily the best way to advertise. Advertising refers specifically to paid forms of promotion, including newspaper, radio, and magazine ads, billboards, brochures, and direct mailing and e-mail. Depending on the advertising budget, this can be contracted out or done in house.

Before embarking on an advertising campaign (self-styled or othewise), answer the following questions:

- What is the advertising objective?

- What is the message you want to send and to whom do you want to send it?

- Does the message reflect the museum's objectives?

- What is the time frame for developing and delivering the message?

- How will you know if you reached the target audience?

Here are a few tips for developing and distributing promotional materials:

- Create a logo that reflects a positive image and use it on all your advertisements.

- Catch the reader's attention within the first three or four seconds.

- Avoid sexist and culturally biased approaches in advertising and promotion.

- Whet learning appetites by letting participants "take the trip" while reading your brochure.

- Mail brochures far enough in advance (ten to sixteen weeks) so that recipients can fit the program into their schedules.

- Avoid mailing around holidays, particularly Christmas.[16]

## Publlicity

Publicity, or unpaid promotion, can help museums with limited budgets reach a broader audience. Perhaps even more than paid advertising, publicity can heighten the visibility of your programs if you think creatively and take action. Publicity may include press releases or public service announcements to local media, fliers posted in strategic spots around town, neighborhood newsletters, industry or trade publications, and exhibits at conferences or fairs. Be sure to take advantage of your own position and insert the museum's brochure on scheduled events into all registration packets and notices.

Ask stakeholders for publicity ideas on each upcoming program. They may have internal communication networks within their own organizations and will gladly spread the word. You can also suggest feature ideas to the local media. LERN strongly recommends thinking in terms of story. Highlight the human interest angle. Point out unusual or trendy courses and interesting teachers. The story doesn't have to focus on the program itself to catch the reader's interest; an article on the subject or teacher of the course can be just as valuable.

### Publicity Partners, Collaborations, and Networks

Given dwindling budgets, using partnerships and collaborations are necessary strategies for many museums and other adult education institutions. Cooperation not only adds resources, but can provide different points of view and connections.

Many adult groups and businesses in the community manage large mailing lists and might be willing to add information to a publication or Web site free of charge. Potential publicity partners may include:

- Chambers of commerce

- Service clubs (for example, Junior League, Scouts, Kiwanis, and Rotary)

- Professional organizations (such as those serving physicians, engineers, and teachers)

- Local libraries, universities, and other public institutions

- Banks, department stores, restaurants, and other businesses

- Senior citizen centers

- Local clubs (gardeners, quilters, and history buffs, for instance)

Our museum and the local chapter of the Lewis and Clark Trail Heritage Foundation cohosted a successful lecture series and also cooperated in promoting the series beforehand. By mailing announcements to club members as well as museum members, the series was much better attended than it would have been had either organization planned it alone. Chapter officers did an excellent job of putting up posters around town, often in places museum staff wouldn't have thought of.

## Publicize, Publicize, Publicize!

- *Create partnerships with instructors and other staff.* As part of the instructor's contract, consider offering financial incentives for recruiting registrants.
- *Invite freelance writers, radio announcers, critics, and other media figures to attend your programs free of charge.* Get to know key media figures in your community and stay in touch with them on a regular basis. These people reach a crowd of potential customers every day. This type of publicity for ongoing adult museum programs is invaluable to sustained success.
- *Organize an "Upcoming Programs" display.* Show off items that course participants have made or show pictures from museum-sponsored trips in an eye-catching exhibit. Make sure the display booth is visible during all museum programs. Create a second display to make the rounds of local businesses or convention centers.
- *Hold open houses.* Invite the community to meet instructors and see some of the exciting projects they will get to participate in. Ask past participants to share some of their valuable museum experiences.
- *Distribute course coupons to volunteers.* Thank your volunteers for their continuing support with a certificate to bring a friend to a future class.
- *Start a member listserv.* Collect e-mail addresses on every registration form. Then send members up-to-date information highlighting current programs and registration information. This information can be reorganized weekly to focus on programs in which registration is lagging.
- *Reward word-of-mouth promoters.* Word of mouth may be one of the most far-reaching and effective methods of publicizing museum programs. Provide incentives or rewards for people who have promoted your programs with a discount certificate they can use for their next museum program.
- *Invite local artists to perform poetry or music relating to an ongoing exhibit.* People who come to see the performer may never have visited the museum before.
- *Public relations or personal contact.* This type of publicity can be unpaid or paid and usually involves someone "talking up" the museum and its programs to prospective participants and supporters. Ask community leaders if they would like you to speak at their organization's next meeting.
- *Incentives.* Offer a free gift or course coupon as reward for early registration, multiple registrations, or promotion of your program.

## Track Your Hits and Misses

How do you know if your marketing and advertising campaign reached the target audience? How do you know which method was the most successful? Simple: measure your results. By keeping careful records of what worked and what didn't, you will be prepared for your next marketing campaign. To keep track:

- *Record how participants learned about your programs and events.* In course evaluations, include a question asking where participants heard about the program. Ask program participants if the institution's image influenced their decision to enroll in programs.

- *Designate a phone line for your advertisements.* Feature this number on all your advertisements, so when people call you have a way of tracking where they learned about a particular program. You may also want to capture this information through your Web site.

- *Direct mail.* Include a self-addressed envelope, reply card, or coupon in all your direct-mail correspondence, marked in a way that allows you to trace individual promotions.

- *See what the competition is doing.* Get on your competitor's mailing list and compare and contrast. How far in advance do they send out their brochures for upcoming events? Are their brochures well designed and easy to read? Where have you seen their advertisements? How do your programs compare in price, location, advertising and marketing strategies, and image?

## Step Eleven: Show Time—Coordination and Presentation

As all program planners know, coordination is often a tiresome and thankless job. However, an efficiently run program has a better chance of success than one that is not. Nothing frustrates program participants more than poor organization. To ensure programs run smoothly and are remembered positively, investigate facilities ahead of time, present some type of orientation to the learning activity, monitor the program while it's in progress, and provide closure to the program. The quality of your overall program is reflected in your attention to detail.

## Facilities

Throw out your folding chairs! The facility should create a comfortable and positive learning environment. Invest in comfortable chairs, comfortable theaters, refreshments, clean bathrooms, and good audiovisual equipment, sound systems, lighting, and atmosphere. Make your teaching environments as comfortable as your home and extend that sense of hospitality with cordiality, thoughtful introductions of instructor and participants, name tags, orientation materials, and ample refreshments.

## Climate Control

Create a positive climate for the program by beginning with an introduction of staff, program objectives, and basic administrative information. Adult education expert Malcolm Knowles feels this is one of the most crucial points in any adult education program: "I am convinced that what happens in the first hour or so of any learning activity (course, seminar, workshop, institute, tutorial, etc.) largely determines how productive the remaining hours will be."[17]

Provide some way of monitoring the program while it's in progress so that quick decisions or changes can be made if necessary. What will you do in case an instructor gets sick or cancels at the last minute? Do you have backup equipment in case of technological failures? A system must be in place that allows coordinators to make necessary adjustments.

## Closure

In closing the program, ensure that all the evaluation information is gathered and thank or recognize participants and instructors. Let participants or other interested parties know where to get more information on the program topic.

Finish up by making sure all equipment is returned, writing thank-you notes to instructors and everyone else involved in the planning process, and writing down what worked and what didn't. Take time to add notes to your participant profiles. Sit down with the contract instructor and review program participant feedback.

## Defining Success

Can attendance be equated with success in adult programs? When a program draws a large crowd, it's easy to argue that the same program, or one like it, should be repeated. However, most educators would readily admit that programs that produce more far-reaching results within a small group of participants may be more "successful" than programs that have little impact on larger numbers of attendees.

Similar arguments can be made for the financial success of adult programs. While education directors and museum administrators may rejoice over profitable programs, excellent programs don't even necessarily break even. Similarly, a lot of time and resources may be dedicated to a program that is ultimately scrapped.

Almost universally, "success" for program planners and participants alike is a positive learning experience. Most importantly, excellent programs provide participants with the skills and opportunity to think on their own and draw personal and meaningful conclusions.

Unique experiences also define excellence for many program planners. Museums are often in a position to offer programs that are not—or could not—be offered by any other institution: behind-the-scenes tours, visits to dig sites, trips abroad guided by renowned experts. These unique experiences help participants directly connect with other cultures, their own culture, and the natural world.

Program participants have additional criteria for measuring success: establishing new relationships, fellowship, engagement with the museum, and personal growth.

### Elements of a Successful Museum Program at the Science Museum of Minnesota

Experiential—Fun and Hands-on

Balance process with content.
Keep the fun in fundamentals.
Stress concept- and inquiry-based learning using real objects and specimens.

Strong Science Advocacy

Advocate science and the scientific "way of knowing" through the understanding of science as knowledge of the natural and human-built world and the processes by which that knowledge is acquired.

*continued*

**Unique**

Use alternative approaches and innovative techniques for presenting, learning, and teaching science.

**Relevant**

Link science with people's everyday lives.

**Interdisciplinary**

Use interdisciplinary connections and multicultural perspectives to enrich learning.

**Accessible**

Communicate the commitment to making science for everyone.
Facilitate access to both the content of science and the participation in science.

**Individualized**

Allow for different learning styles and abilities.
Encourage intergenerational learning opportunities.

## Step Twelve: Evaluation and Analysis of Learner Outcomes

Clearly, no museum can thrive without knowing what adults want and expect from their museum experience. Evaluations help planners learn exactly that, and are therefore crucial to the success of any program. Program evaluations can help planners determine if program goals and objectives were met, while educational evaluations can be used to assess learning objectives, instructional process, and learning environment. The key to a successful program evaluation is to build support and to involve those people who may be affected by the results. Ideally, evaluation is a continuous, interactive process that is responsive to the issues and concerns of those involved.[18]

The evaluation process can start before the program begins. To get baseline data for planning new programs, participants may be asked to tell (orally or in writing) what they already know about the topic, they may be given a test, or they may be asked to demonstrate a skill.[19] We also observed many instructors asking program participants at the beginning of a session what their personal goals were or what they wanted to gain from the program.

A *formative* evaluation occurs while a program is in progress and can be extremely helpful in determining what changes may be needed to enhance the learning process. Program evaluators can collect information during the program by administering short opinion evaluation forms or quizzes. Crispin and Rampp suggest that the participant group select representatives to meet briefly with instructional leaders at regular intervals during the program to discuss any concerns.[20]

A *summative* evaluation is conducted at the conclusion of the learning event and focuses on results or outcomes. This is the most commonly used evaluation method and usually takes the form of opinion questionnaires. It is important to keep the information from these evaluations as permanent records so they can be used in future planning sessions. One good evaluation tool we encountered was B.E.R.T. (Better Education through Revenue and Tracking), developed by the St. Louis Science Center.

Besides simply informing planners if participants liked a particular program, Fellenz, Conti, and Seaman[1] suggest program evaluations can also:

- Provide information for decision-making on all aspects of the program.
- Increase application of the learning by participants and anyone else interested in the program.
- Meet requirements of the program sponsor (to become or remain accountable).
- Provide a feeling of worth or accomplishment to the program staff.
- Provide data on the major accomplishments of the program.
- Describe what happened so that other educators can determine if they wish to duplicate the program.
- Facilitate decisions related to program improvement and future operation.

1. Robert Fellenz, Gary Conti, and Don Seaman, "Evaluate: Student, Staff, Program," in *Materials and Methods in Adult and Continuing Education*, edited by C. Klevins (Los Angeles: Kleven, 1982), 333–45.

### Suggestions for Developing Useful and Constructive Evaluations

Evaluations can be spur of the moment or they can take a more systematic approach, such as formal needs assessment. Whatever method you decide to use, let these steps and suggestions be a guide:

- *How and Who?* Specify how the program will be evaluated. Will existing staff evaluate the program or will a consulting firm be brought in? An observation protocol that you can use is found in appendix E.

- *What and When?* Determine standards or criteria by which to judge program objectives. For example, what are program participants expected to learn and how will they use that learning? When the criteria have been established, communicate them clearly to everyone involved. Discuss evaluation criteria at the beginning of the activity so expectations are clear.

- *Pick an Approach.* Determine the most appropriate approach to your evaluation. Techniques used for generating program ideas, for example, questionnaires, surveys, interviews, tests, observations, portfolios, and performance reviews, can also be adapted to the evaluation process.

- *K.I.S.S.* "Keep It Simple." Evaluation questions should be specific and should request only one piece of information. Keep evaluations as short as possible.

- *Make Time, Make Everybody.* Ensure that the evaluation is a scheduled part of the program and that all individuals who took part in the program, including participants, instructors, administrators, and service providers, complete the evaluation.

- *Reassure and Respond.* Make sure respondents know that the information will be reviewed, but that it will remain anonymous. Respond to the recommendations and communicate the final suggestions to all parties. Let those who were involved know they have been heard and let them know how the results will be used for developing future programs.

- *And the Answer Is?* Based on the predetermined criteria, decide whether the program was successful or not. Present recommendations for current or future programs, including what resources will be needed.

## The Transference of Learning and Analysis of Learner Outcomes

Evaluations conducted immediately at the conclusion of programs are very useful. (A standard evaluation form is found in appendix C.) However, follow-up surveys conducted later can more accurately determine if program participants have found ways to apply what they've learned. This successful "transference of learning" is the hallmark of an excellent program. If an institution is seriously engaged in improving the quality of people's lives, this outcome evaluation is essential. Also, some funding agencies or employers may want evidence that learners used the information.

Michael Spock has theorized that learner outcomes may change additionally over longer periods of time. In a panel discussion, "On Beyond Now: Strategies for Assessing the Long Term Impact of Museum Experiences," Spock used a chart to illustrate that learner outcomes may change over time and the tradeoffs this suggests for both influencing and assessing those evolving outcomes.[21] We concur. Awareness of learner outcomes is critical to designing meaningful life-changing experiences both in the short and long term.

Participants are more likely to be able to answer questions relating to transference of learning if they are questioned six to eight weeks after the program, instead of immediately after. This allows participants time to assess the experience and find ways to apply information. Delayed evaluations also provide a better measure of learner outcomes. (From base to apex, the pyramid of learner outcomes is knowledge or skill mastery, expanded relationships, increased appreciation or meaningfulness, changed attitudes or emotions, transformed perspectives, and life-changing experiences. See chapter 1 for more on learner outcomes.) A long-term learner outcomes survey form can be found in appendix D.

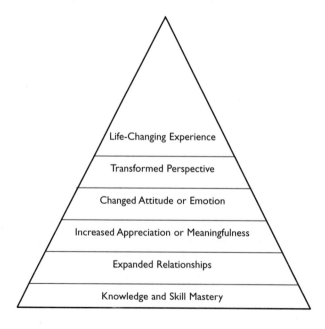

**Table 6.1.    Contrasting Learning Outcomes and Research Strategies**

| *Straightforward Outcomes:* <br> *Data Collected Sooner* | *More Profound Outcomes:* <br> *Data Collected Later* |
|---|---|
| Expectations of relatively direct, immediate impcts | Expectations of relatively complex, evolving impacts. |
| Experience is probably easier to design and program. | Experience may be much harder to design and program |
| Museum may be more likely to influence the outcomes. | Museum may be less likely to influence the outcomes. |
| Data is more readily and directly linked to the museum experience. | Data is less readily and directly linked to the museum experience. |
| Subject's memories of experience are fresher. | Subject's memories of experience may be fainter. |
| There is less time for the external environment to influence and the subject to reconstruct memories of the museum experience. | There is more time for the external environment to influence and the subject to reconstruct memories of the museum experience. |
| There is a low dilution factor, so effects are more likely to be detected among the study's subjects. | There is a high dilution factor, so effects are less likely to be detected in the general population. |
| Learning is apt to be more objectively reported and measured, but less emotionally rich. | Learning is apt to be more subjectively reported, emotionally rich, and harder to measure. |
| Learning detected immediately may not be lasting. | Learning detected later is, by definition, lasting. |
| We are likely to be able to make a convincing case for more profound outcomes from the learning experience. | We may be able to make a convincing case for more profound outcomes from the learning experience. |

*Note:* Awareness of learner outcomes is critical to designing meaningful life-changing experiences both in the short and long terms. Michael Spock's chart illustrates how learner outcomes may change over time. It also points up trade-offs in influencing and assessing those evolving outcomes.

*Source:* Michael Spock, "On Beyond Now: Strategies for Assessing the Long Term Impact of Museum Experiences" (panel discussion at the American Association of Museums Conference, Baltimore, Md., 2000).

Consider calling a select number of program participants six to eight weeks after a program and asking them what they remember. How have they used any of the information from the program?

Have they since talked with anyone from the program? Has the program inspired them to buy a book? Pursue similar interests? Have they shared what they learned with anyone else? Was the program a life-changing experience? Experiment with some new tools. A minimum of six weeks after an experience, pick up the phone. Gain some insights into the personal *impacts* your programs have.

## Last but Not Least: Communicate the Value of the Program

Now that you have planned, advertised, delivered, and evaluated your successful adult program, what's next? You may decide at this point that you have enough information about the success or failure of your programs and can now take a breath. However, some of those all-important stakeholders or funding agencies may want some sort of accountability for their efforts and funding. Certainly, other program planners would be interested in learning what worked in preparing, promoting, and delivering your programs. Here are two examples of ways in which to communicate the value of your program:

- Host an open house and invite other educational institutions to share their successful adult education programs. Work with these people in developing a Web site or other bulletin boards to share ideas.

- Prepare a report for key individuals or groups. The type of report will depend on the purpose of the report, what you want to say, and to whom you want to say it. For example, if you are using the report to gain support for current or future programs from community leaders or advisory board members, Rosemary Caffarella suggests considering presenting selected parts of the program either orally or in writing.[22]

## The Creative Art of Creating Excellent Experiences

People generally think of museums as places where collections are gathered, stored, and displayed for the education and enjoyment of the public. Human minds can also be thought of as museums—places where images, ideas, and visions are gathered, cared for, and processed into words and action. The art of the museum educator is to care for these "museums of the minds" as attentively as they care for the physical museums in which they labor. Developing purposeful learning experiences is a critical part of this work.

This book is our invitation—challenge, if you will—to program planners to strive to create programs that are meaningful educational experiences for participants, experiences that, in turn, challenge learners to create new meaning for their own lives. We don't presume this will be easy; we simply presume that it will be worthy.

## Notes

1. Jack Mezirow, *Transformative Dimensions of Adult Learning* (San Francisco: Jossey-Bass, 1991), 8.

2. Rosemary Caffarella, *Planning Programs for Adult Learners* (San Francisco: Jossey-Bass, 1994), 49.

3. Caffarella, *Programs for Adult Learners*, 47.

4. Conversation with Laura Sadowski, development director, Strong Museum.

5. Alan Knox, *Helping Adults Learn: A Guide to Planning, Implementing, and Conducting Programs* (San Francisco: Jossey-Bass, 1986), 72.

6. B. Joseph Pine, "Interview: B. Joseph Pine—Experience Required," interview by Meridith Levinson, *CIO Magazine*, November 15, 1999, 2.

7. J. K. Broomall and R. B. Fischer, "Budgeting Techniques in Continuing Education," in *Organization and Administration of Continuing Education: A Textbook Designed to Facilitate Successful Programs and Processes in Adult and Continuing Education*, edited by V. W. Mott and L. C. Rampp, 277–302 (Checotah, Okla.: AP Publications, 1995), 284.

8. Caffarella, *Programs for Adult Learners*, 168–69.

9. L. J. Davis, "Marketing Techniques in Continuing Education," in *Organization and Administration of Continuing Education: A Textbook Designed to Facilitate Successful Programs and Processes in Adult and Continuing Education*, edited by V. W. Mott and L. C. Rampp, 303–334 (Checotah, Okla.: AP Publications, 1995), 321.

10. R. G. Simerly and Associates, ed., *Handbook of Marketing Continuing Education* (San Francisco: Jossey-Bass, 1989), 59.

11. Julie Coates, "Marketing Recreation Classes Meeting the Criteria for Excellence: How Do You Rate?" *LERN Newsletter* (March 1999).

12. Davis, "Marketing Techniques," 332.

13. Davis, "Marketing Techniques," 316.

14. Conversation with Laura Sadowski.

15. Alan Knox, "Adults as Learners," *Museum News* 59, no. 5 (1981): 28.

16. R. G. Simerly and Associates, ed., *Handbook*, 289.

17. Malcolm Knowles, *The Adult Learner: An Endangered Species* (Houston: Gulf, 1973), 224.

18. Robert Fellenz, Gary Conti, and Don Seaman, "Evaluate: Student, Staff, Program," in *Materials and Methods in Adult Education*, edited by C. Klevins (Los Angeles: Kleven, 1982), 339.

19. E. A. Crispin and L. C. Rampp, "Evaluation Methods for Use in Continuing Education," in *Organization and Administration of Continuing Education: A Textbook Designed to Facilitate Successful Programs and Processes in Adult and Continuing Education*, edited by V. W. Mott and L. C. Rampp, 214–43 (Checotah, Okla.: AP Publications, 1995), 232.

20. Crispin and Rampp, "Evaluation Methods," 232.

21. Michael Spock, "On Beyond Now: Strategies for Assessing the Long Term Impact of Museum Experiences" (panel discussion notes, American Association of Museums Conference, Baltimore, Md., 2000).

22. Caffarella, *Programs for Adult Learners*, 232.

# INSTRUCTOR'S GUIDE SHEET

Museum name
Museum address
Museum telephone
Museum e-mail
Museum Web site

Thank you for agreeing to teach one of our adult programs. You represent the most important link between our museum and the adult participants.

**Our goal is to create excellent learning experiences here that change adult lives in positive and significant ways.** To help you do this, the education department has collected some ideas, tips, and suggestions that work well in teaching adult programs. We've listed some of these recommendations below.

## Museum Links

1. With each workshop:

   - Explain who you are and why you are giving this program.

   - Provide an overview and agenda for your class.

   - Explain how your program relates to the Museum.

   - Provide handouts or something participants can take home with them.

   - Please check with the program coordinator to see if there is any research published by the Museum that pertains to your class. We will be glad to make copies of related articles for you and your workshop participants.

- Throughout the class, promote interaction among the participants.

- Provide a question-and-answer period.

- Share information with participants about where they can learn more about your subject matter.

- Provide an initial orientation session that overviews your class.

- Attempt to be the type of instructor who is a facilitator, flexible to the needs of your learners, and enthusiastic about your subject.

- Remember that teaching isn't talking; it's helping people learn.

2. When teaching adult programs, please utilize the Museum resources as much as possible. We encourage you to focus your workshop on an exhibit or display within the Museum. We do have teaching collections and you can find out about the location of these by calling the Programs Coordinator at 555-5555. If appropriate, we also encourage you to take your class onto the Museum floor.

3. All of our adult programs are linked to the mission of this Museum. The mission of this Museum is to enhance visitor understanding of the natural and cultural world. As you are outlining your workshop, please link it in as many ways as possible to our mission.

## Logistics

4. You'll be teaching in the classroom located at the lower level of the Museum. It contains (1) circular, moveable 6-ft. diameter tables and chairs, (2) 3-ft. by 18-ft. white board, (3) one sink, (4) TV and VCR, (5) TV cable link up, (6) various art supplies, paper, scissors, crayons, etc. (located in the drawers and cabinets). The Museum has other audiovisual equipment that can be obtained by calling the Programs Coordinator at 555-5555.

5. Report any daytime emergencies that occur during class to the person at the information desk located inside the office area. The information desk also has some minor first-aid supplies.

6. When a class is held in the Museum, participants are to check in at the main lobby desk before they come to the classroom. You will be given a class roster at that time. Plan to utilize the complete time period that your class is scheduled for.

## Evaluation

7. We ask that you distribute standard evaluation forms to all participants at the end of your workshop. Staff may also call participants several weeks after a workshop is over to assess its impact. Copies of these forms will be given to you upon completion of the course as well. We will also ask you to fill out an instructor evaluation form.

**Thanks again for creating an excellent learning experience! We hope you enjoy your experience as much as we appreciate you taking the time to teach this class!**

# LETTER OF CONTRACT EXAMPLE

Name of Contract Employee: _____

This is your offer of contract from the Museum.

Class Title: _____

Date of Class: _____Time of Class: _____

## Section I
## Instructor Expectations

An abstract on the program will be sent to the Museum no later than one week after the Contract Employee has agreed to do the program for the Museum. The abstract will include:

- Title of the program;

- At least two dates and times that you could teach the program;

- Abstract of no more than 50 words on the program;

- Age group for participants;

- Whether a materials fee must be charged or not (if so, the cost);

- Short bio that explains your background and why you're teaching this course.

The Contract Employee agrees to perform the following:

- Development of class activities, including initial planning;

- Preparation of all materials needed;

- Purchasing all materials needed with the assistance of the Education Department;

- Utilizing our objectives as listed in the class description during the established time of the class;

- Restoring the room used to its original condition prior to the start of the class;

- Reporting any damages that occurred to Museum property during the class to the Education Department.

All programs and content must meet the standards established by the Director of Education and his/her designee. These standards include:

- Provide stimulating informal learning programs that encourage persons of all ages to participate in learning experiences outside the formal classroom;

- Provide cognitive, affective, psychological, and social learning experiences using real objects as the salient materials where possible;

- Orient museum visitors to the Mission;

- Build on visitors' current knowledge base and previous experience;

- Inspire learning in visitors of all ages;

- Raise awareness of new ideas by sharing current research;

- Cultivate scientific thinking skills.

## Section II
## Consideration

For your teaching assignment, you will be reimbursed at the rate of $_____.___ per hour. This appointment is contingent on class registration reaching its stated minimum. In the event that the class does not have sufficient enrollment, this appointment may be terminated at the option of the Museum.

The Museum agrees to pay the Contract Employee the above sum for satisfactory completion of the contracted service.

The Museum agrees to pay this amount to the Contract Employee within sixty days of the last class.

## Section III
## Contract Termination

This contract may be terminated in writing at any time by either party.

## Section IV
## Relationship

The parties to this Agreement intend that the relationship between them created by this contract is that of the Contract Employee and not an employee of the Museum. For the purpose of this contract, the Contract Employee is not subject to the supervision and control of the Museum, nor is the Contract Employee carrying out the regular business of the Museum. Each of the parties will be solely and entirely responsible for their own acts and/or the acts of their employees. No benefits provided by the Museum to its employees, including but not limited to unemployment and workers' compensation insurance, are available to the Contract Employee.

## Section V
## Process for Modification

This instrument contains the entire Agreement between the parties and no statements, promised or in document form, by either party or agents of either party which are not contained in this written Agreement are valid or binding. This Agreement may not be enlarged, modified, or altered except in writing, signed by all parties to this Agreement.

## Section VI
## Indemnity

The Contract Employee hereof agrees to hold harmless the Museum and the State of Montana from all claims and liability due to the activity of the Contract Employee and his/her agents and/or employees.

If the offer of appointment and terms of this contract are satisfactory, please sign one copy of this letter (keep the other for your files) and return to:

EDUCATION DIRECTOR
MUSEUM
ADDRESS

Date                                    Education Director

Date                                    Name of Contract Employee

(Date) _____

(Education Director) _____

(Date) _____

(Name of Contract Employee) _____

This contract is made and entered into between the Museum and

(Contract Employee) _____

(Address) _____

(City/State/Zip) _____

(Phone Number) _____

# GENERAL ADULT PROGRAM EVALUATION FORM
## (to be distributed at the end of a program)

**Museum Name**
**Museum Class**
**Date**
**Evaluation Form**

*Please take a few moments to complete this evaluation. Your comments will help us plan similar classes in the future. Thank you.*

*Please use the following scale to rate these questions:*

**1 = Excellent    2 = Good    3 = Fair    4 = Poor    5 = Needs Improvement**

_____    How well did the instructor communicate her/his subject?

_____    How well did the instructor keep your interest in the subject?

_____    How well did the instructor encourage participation with others?

_____    How well did the course meet your expectations?

_____    How would you rate the facilities?

_____    How would you rate staff assistance and friendliness?

Overall, were you satisfied with the class?        _____ Yes        _____ No

If you answered no, why?

_____

_____

Is there anything about the class that you would have changed? _____ Yes _____ No

If you answered yes, what?

_____

_____

Are you a member of the Museum?               _____ Yes          _____ No

How often do you attend the Museum or participate in Museum programs or classes?

_____ Never   _____ Seldom (1–5 times a year)

_____ Frequently (6–12 times a year)   _____ Often (13+ times a year)

If you answered Never or Seldom, why?

_____

_____

How did you learn about this class?

_____ Museum Mailing   _____ Newspaper   _____ Radio

_____ Friend or Relative   _____ Other:

_____

**Thank you for taking the time to complete this evaluation.**

# PHONE INTERVIEW SURVEY FORM

For Measuring Long-Term Learner Outcomes (for use by education department staff with program participants six to eight weeks after the program is completed)

## Motivation

Why did you decide to participate in this program?

Which of the following statements best describes your situation:

I wanted to participate in this program

____ to gain new knowledge (knowledge seekers)
____ to learn a new skill (skill builders)
____ to meet and get to know other adults (socializers)
____ to spend time at the Museum with friends (museum lovers)

Did you have an interest in the subject beforehand? Can you describe other programs, activities, or experiences that you have had related to the subject? How long ago were those experiences?

## Measuring Learning

What do you remember about this program?

What would you tell a friend about this program?

Do you think it has changed or will change you in any way? (e.g., you used the knowledge, bought a book, talked to others about what you learned)

## Outcomes

(Based on our learner outcomes taxonomy)

Did this program:

____ enable you to acquire and use new information?

____ help you make new friends, develop community contacts, or share ideas with family, friends, and coworkers?

____ foster a deeper appreciation of the arts and sciences?

____ help you feel more self-confident or personally grow or change in any way?

____ cause you to examine your ideas about how the world works or fundamentally change your understanding of the world?

____ change your life in any way?

Do you think this experience has changed what you do today? This month? Next year?

How valuable was this experience for you?

## Demographics

**Gender** ____ Female     ____ Male;     **Age** _____

What is the highest **level of education** you have obtained?

____Grade School    ____High School    ____Some College

____College Grad    ____Postgraduate

**Occupation** _____

Are you a member of this Museum?    ____Yes    ____No

Have you attended other adult programs at this Museum? ____Yes ____No

Thank you for taking the time to talk with me this evening. I hope you will have an opportunity to come back to the Museum soon and participate in another adult program.

# ADULT PROGRAM OBSERVATION PROTOCOL

This general evaluation tool is designed to assist an educator in personally evaluating adult programs, exhibits, tours, or other educational activities. It includes segments for comments on the program, the leader(s), and the participants, but it relies on the observer's discretion in interpreting the value of what is occurring.

Name of Program/Course _____

Name of Instructor _____

Number of Participants _____

Name of Observer _____ Date_____

## General Description of Events of Program/Course

### General Comments
### Observations of Programs

Orientation. Was there a suitable orientation or introduction to the content so that participants could relate to what was happening? Were the general atmosphere and physical setting comfortable?

Strengths/Weaknesses. Describe things that went well or give an example of an "illuminative moment." What were the things that did not "work well" regarding the activity, the instructor, the management, the environment, or other aspects of the program?

## Observations of Learners

(Check the frequency with which you observed the following levels of learning and add any appropriate comments.)

### Knowledge/Comprehension

(Evidenced by learner actions such as active listening, note taking, requests for clarification, or casual reading or observing)

Never ____ Seldom ____ Occasionally ____ Frequently ____

### Application/Analysis

(Evidenced by learner actions such as applying information, trying out, questioning, giving examples, concentrated reading, or observing)

Never ____ Seldom ____ Occasionally ____ Frequently ____

### Synthesis/Evaluation

(Evidenced by learner actions such as expressing like or dislike, revising, modeling, or insightful group discussion)

Never ____ Seldom ____ Occasionally ____ Frequently ____

Were sources of further information available or noted? Did the program seem to stimulate further interest in the topic? How?

How did the program relate to the purpose of the Museum? Did it make use of collections or local resources?

## Observations of Teachers/Leaders (Add comments as appropriate)

1. The leader's approach appeared to be learner centered.

| 1 | 2 | 3 | 4 | 5 |
|---|---|---|---|---|

Very little                                  Very much

2. The program did seem to meet the learners' needs and interests.

| 1 | 2 | 3 | 4 | 5 |
|---|---|---|---|---|

Very little                                  Very much

3. Material presented related to the level of experience of the group.

| 1 | 2 | 3 | 4 | 5 |
|---|---|---|---|---|

Very little                                  Very much

4. Learner needs were assessed or given consideration.

| 1 | 2 | 3 | 4 | 5 |
|---|---|---|---|---|

Very little                                  Very much

5. Dialogue and interaction indicated a comfortable atmosphere.

| 1 | 2 | 3 | 4 | 5 |
|---|---|---|---|---|

Very little                                  Very much

6. Self-direction rather than teacher domination was evident.

| 1 | 2 | 3 | 4 | 5 |
|---|---|---|---|---|

Very little                                  Very much

7. The leader was a facilitator rather than a presenter.

| 1 | 2 | 3 | 4 | 5 |
|---|---|---|---|---|

Very little                                  Very much

8. The leader and program were well prepared.

| 1 | 2 | 3 | 4 | 5 |
|---|---|---|---|---|

Very little                                             Very much


9. Teaching methods appropriate to various learning styles were used.

| 1 | 2 | 3 | 4 | 5 |
|---|---|---|---|---|

Very little                                             Very much


10. Leaders were enthused about the topic and liked teaching it.

| 1 | 2 | 3 | 4 | 5 |
|---|---|---|---|---|

Very little                                             Very much

# PARTICIPANT PROFILE

Name _____  No. of years living in the community____

Spouse's Name _____

Involvement with Museum as a

Address_____  ____ member

E-mail _____  ____ patron

____ volunteer

Phone_____  ____ board member

Employment _____

Interests and Hobbies

_____

_____

Spouse's interests and hobbies

_____

_____

Museum programs both have participated in:                    Year

_____

_____

_____

_____

_____

What other organizations is this person currently involved with?

_____

_____

Friends at Museum                    E-mail

_____

_____

_____

_____

_____

_____

Last updated _____
By _____

**What types of programs do you provide at your museum for the four types of adult learners?**

## Knowledge Seekers

* Desire to learn
* Learning is FUN!
* Social aspect not as important

_____

_____

_____

_____

_____

## Museum Lovers

* Love being at the Museum
* Want to be with those of similar
  interests

_____

_____

_____

_____

_____

## Skill Builders

* Want to learn a skill and take
  something home
* Social aspect varies from
  somewhat to very important

_____

_____

_____

_____

_____

## Socializers

* Want to socialize with friends,
  family, and meet new people
  Subgroup: Tag-alongs
* Friend/family member attends (sometimes they are interested, sometimes
  not)

_____

_____

_____

_____

_____

# PROGRAM PLANNER WORKSHEET

What are the barriers and constraints to offering adult programs in your museum?

Money

_____

_____

_____

Staff

_____

_____

_____

Space and Equipment

_____

_____

_____

Marketing and Promotion

_____

_____

_____

Increased Competition

_____

_____

_____

Diverse Audience Needs

_____

_____

_____

Other

_____

_____

_____

_____

Other

_____

_____

_____

_____

**What do you look for in choosing adult education instructors?**

*Museum program planners typically look for instructors who can wear at least four hats: programmer, guide, content resource, and institutional representative.*

Experience/Credibility

_____

_____

_____

Credentials

_____

_____

_____

Teaching Ability/Style

_____

_____

_____

Good Communication Skills

_____

_____

_____

Museum Experience

_____

_____

_____

Availability

_____

_____

_____

Other

_____

_____

_____

_____

_____

Other

_____

_____

_____

_____

_____

**What types of support do you provide your instructors?**

_____

_____

_____

_____

_____

_____

**Why?**

_____

_____

_____

_____

_____

_____

| What types of support would you like to be providing your instructors? | Why? |
|---|---|
| _____ | _____ |
| _____ | _____ |
| _____ | _____ |
| _____ | _____ |
| _____ | _____ |

## Finding Direction

What are your core values (guiding principles)?

What kinds of learning experiences do you want adults to have?

What are the unique characteristics of your programs?

## Goal Setting

What is the mission of your education department?
(who you are, what you do, and who you serve)

What is your vision for your adult museum programs?
(where will you be in three years—write in the future tense)

## Implementation

What are the top ten things that you want every instructor to do when they are teaching a class at your museum?

1.

2.

3.

4.

5.

6.

7.

8.

9.

10.

What are the top ten logistical issues that instructors need to know about in order to successfully teach in your museum?

1.

2.

3.

4.

5.

6.

7.

8.

9.

10.

In what ways do you currently provide access to unique people, places, and things in your museum?

How would you like to expand access to unique people, places, and things in the future?

How will you "brand" your adult museum programs?

Write a description for a future adult experience in your museum that reflects your core values and brand.

# BIBLIOGRAPHY

American Association of Museums, ed. *Excellence and Equity: Education and the Public Dimension of Museums.* Washington, D.C.: American Association of Museums, 1992.

Ansbacher, T. "John Dewey's 'Experience and Education': Lessons for Museums." *Curator* 41, no. 1 (1998): 36–49.

Aslanian, Carol, and Henry Brickell. *Americans in Transition: Life Changes as Reasons for Adult Learning.* New York: College Entrance Examination Board, 1980.

Bankirer, M. "Adjunct Faculty as Integrated Resources in Continuing Education." In *Organization and Administration of Continuing Education: A Textbook Designed to Facilitate Successful Programs and Processes in Adult and Continuing Education,* edited by V. W. Mott and L. C. Rampp, 135–43. Checotah, Okla.: AP Publications, 1995.

Bloom, Joel N., and Ann Mintz. "Museums and the Future of Education." *Journal of Museum Education* 14, no. 3 (fall 1990): 71–78.

Bogdan, Robert C., and Sari Biklen. *Qualitative Research for Education: An Introduction to Theory and Methods.* Boston: Allyn and Bacon, 1992.

Borun, Minda, M. Cleghorn, and A. Chambers. "Families Are Learning in Science Museums." *Curator* 39, no. 2 (1996): 123–38.

Brockett, Ralph G., and Roger Hiemstra. "Philosophical and Ethical Considerations." In *Program Planning for the Training and Continuing Education of Adults,* edited by Peter S. Cookson, 115–33. Malabar, Fla.: Krieger, 1998.

Brookfield, Stephen. *Understanding and Facilitating Adult Learning.* San Francisco: Jossey-Bass, 1986.

Broomall, J. K., and R. B. Fischer. "Budgeting Techniques in Continuing Education." In *Organization and Administration of Continuing Education: A Textbook Designed to Facilitate Successful Programs and Processes in Adult and Continuing Education,* edited by V. W. Mott and L. C. Rampp, 277–302. Checotah, Okla.: AP Publications, 1995.

Brown, Ellsworth. "Catalogue of Change." *Museum News* 76, no. 6 (1997): 39–40.

Brown, L. "An Adult Educator's Perspective." In *Museums and the Education of Adults*, edited by A. Chadwick and A. Staten. Leicester, England: National Institute of Adult Continuing Education, 1995.

Buck, C. "How to Work with an Advertising Agency." In *Handbook of Marketing for Continuing Education,* edited by R. G. Simerly, 286–94. San Francisco: Jossey-Bass, 1989.

Caffarella, Rosemary S. *Planning Programs for Adult Learners.* San Francisco: Jossey-Bass, 1994.

Carr, David. "The Adult Learner in the Museum." In *Museums and Universities: New Paths for Continuing Education,* edited by J. W. Solinger. New York: Collier Macmillan, 1990.

Caston, Ellie B. "A Model for Teaching in a Museum Setting." In *Museum Education: History, Theory, and Practice,* edited by N. Berry and S. Mayer, 90–108. Reston, Va.: National Art Education Association, 1989.

Chadwick, A., and A. Stannett, eds. *Museums and the Education of Adults.* Leicester, England: National Organization for Adult Learning, 1995.

Chesebrough, David. "Museum Partnerships: Insights from the Literature and Research." *Museum News* 77, no. 6 (1998): 53.

Coates, Julie. "Marketing Recreation Classes Meeting the Criteria for Excellence: How Do You Rate? *LERN Newsletter* (March 1999).

*The Condition of Education 2000.* Washington, D.C.: National Center for Education Statistics, 2000.

Conti, Gary J. "The Relationship between Teaching Style and Adult Student Learning." *Adult Education Quarterly* 35, no. 4 (1985): 220–28.

———. "Assessing Teaching Style in Continuing Education. In *New Directions for Continuing Education,* no. 43, edited by R. G. Brockett and A. B. Knox. San Francisco: Jossey-Bass, 1989.

Crispin, E. A., and L. C. Rampp. "Evaluation Methods for Use in Continuing Education." In *Organization and Administration of Continuing Education: A Textbook Designed to Facilitate Successful Programs and Processes in Adult and Continuing Education,* edited by V. W. Mott and L. C. Rampp, 214–43. Checotah, Okla.: AP Publications, 1995.

Csikszentmihalyi, Mihaly, and Kim Hermanson. "Intrinsic Motivation in Museums: What Makes Visitors Want to Learn?" In *Public Institutions for Personal Learning: Establishing a Research Agenda,* edited by J. H. Falk and L. D. Dierking, 67–77. Washington, D.C.: American Association of Museums, 1995. *Museum News* 74, no. 3 (1995): 35.

Davis, L. J. "Marketing Techniques in Continuing Education." In *Organization and Administration of Continuing Education: A Textbook Designed to Facilitate Successful Programs and Processes in Adult and Continuing Education,* edited by V. W. Mott and L. C. Rampp, 303–334. Checotah, Okla: AP Publications, 1995.

Deshler, David. "Measurement and Appraisal of Program Success." In *Program Planning for the Training and Continuing Education of Adults,* edited by Peter S. Cookson, 301–328. Malabar, Fla.: Krieger, 1998.

Diamond, Judy. "The Behavior of Family Groups in Science Museums." *Curator* 29, no. 2 (1986): 139–54.

———. *Practical Evaluation Guide.* Walnut Creek, Calif.: AltaMira, 1999.

Eggen, D. "A Taste of Slavery Has Tourists up in Arms." *Washington Post,* 7 July 1999, A1, A9.

Falk, John H. "Toward a Better Understanding of Why People Go to Museums," *Museum News* (1998): 38–43.

Falk, John, and Lynn Dierking. "Recalling the Museum Experience." In *Transforming Practice: Selections from the* Journal of Museum Education *1992–1999,* edited by J. S. Hirsch and L. H. Silverman, 268–77. Washington, D.C.: Museum Education Roundtable, 2000.

Fellenz, Robert, and Gary Conti. "Learning and Reality: Reflections on Trends in Adult Learning." *ERIC Clearinghouse on Adult, Career, and Vocational Education,* 7–11. Columbus: Ohio State University, 1989.

Fellenz, Robert, Gary Conti, and Don Seaman. "Evaluate: Student, Staff, Program." In *Materials and Methods in Adult and Continuing Education,* edited by C. Klevins, 342. Los Angeles: Kleven, 1982.

Freire, Paulo. *Pedagogy of the Oppressed.* New York: Herder and Herder, 1970.

Futter, Ellen. "Biodiversity." *Museum News* 76, no. 6 (1997): 40–42.

Graham, Angela. "Persistence without External Rewards: A Study of Adult Learners in Art Museum and Planetarium Education Programs." Ph.D. diss., Northern Illinois University, 1990.

Guba, Egon. *Toward a Methodology of Naturalistic Inquiry in Education Evaluation.* Los Angeles: University of California, Center for the Study of Evaluation, 1978.

Hein, G. E., and M. Alexander. *Museums: Places of Learning.* Washington, D.C.: American Association of Museums, Education Committee, 1998.

Hiemstra, Roger. "The State of the Art." In S*elected Reprints from Museums, Adults and the Humanities: A Guide for Educational Programming,* 38–50. Washington, D.C.: American Association of Museums, 1993.

Hood, M. G., and L. C. Roberts. "Neither Too Young nor Too Old: A Comparison of Visitor Characteristics." *Curator* 37, no. 1 (1994): 36–45.

Hood, Marilyn. "Adult Attitudes toward Leisure Choices in Relation to Museum Participation." Ph.D. diss., Ohio State University, 1981.

———. "Leisure Criteria of Family Participation and Nonparticipation in Museums." *Marriage and Family Review* 13, no. 4 (1989): 151–69.

Horn, Adrianne. "Much More from California: Lecture vs. Discussion—The Adult Tour Dilemma." *Museum Education Roundtable Reports* 4, no. 4 (1979): 1–4.

Hughes, Catherine. *Museum Theatre.* Portsmouth, N.H.: Heinemann, 1998.

Hyman, Mary. *Adult Education Survey.* Washington, D.C.: Association of Science-Technology Centers, 1976.

Knowles, Malcolm. *The Adult Learner: A Neglected Species.* Houston: Gulf, 1973.

———. *What Is Andragogy? Modern Practice of Adult Education.* 2d ed. Chicago: Association Press, 1980.

Knox, Alan. "Adults as Learners." *Museum News* 59, no. 5 (1981): 24–29.

————. *Helping Adults Learn: A Guide to Planning, Implementing, and Conducting Programs*. San Francisco: Jossey-Bass, 1986.

————. *Helping Adults Learn: A Guide to Planning, Implementing, and Conducting Programs*. San Francisco: Jossey-Bass, 1990.

Lamdin, Lois. *Elderlearning: New Frontier in an Aging Society*. Phoenix: Oryx, 1997.

Leichter, Hope, and Michael Spock. "Learning from Ourselves: Pivotal Stories of Museum Professionals." In *Bridges to Understanding Children's Museums*, edited by Nina Gibans, 41–83. Cleveland: Mandel Center for Nonprofit Organizations, Case Western Reserve University, 1999.

McCoy, Sue. "Docents in Art Museum Education." In *Museum Education: History, Theory, and Practice*, edited by N. Berry and S. Mayer, 135–53. Reston, Va.: National Art Education Association, 1989.

Merriam, Sharon. *Case Study Research in Education: A Qualitative Approach*. San Francisco: Jossey-Bass, 1988.

Merriam, Sharon, and Rosemary Caffarella. *Learning in Adulthood*. San Francisco: Jossey-Bass 1991.

Mezirow, Jack. *Transformative Dimensions of Adult Learning*. San Francisco: Jossey-Bass, 1991.

————. "Understanding Transformation Theory." *Adult Education Quarterly* 44, no. 4 (1994): 222–26.

————. "Contemporary Paradigms of Learning." *Adult Education Quarterly* 46, no. 3 (1996): 158–73.

————. "On Critical Reflection." *Adult Education Quarterly* 48, no. 3 (1998): 185–98.

National Center for Education Statistics. *Adult Education Survey*. Washington, D.C.: National Center for Education Statistics, 1998.

Pine, B. Joseph. "Interview: B. Joseph Pine—Experience Required." Interview by Meridith Levinson. *CIO Magazine*, 15 November 1999, 3.

Pine, B. Joseph, and James H. Gilmore. "The Experience Economy." *Museum News* 78, no. 2 (1999).

Roberts, Lisa C. *From Knowledge to Narrative: Educators and the Changing Museum*. Washington, D.C.: Smithsonian Institution Press, 1997.

Sachatello-Sawyer, Bonnie. "Coming of Age: The Status of Adult Education Methodology in Museums." Ed.D. diss., Montana State University, 1996.

Sakofs, M. S. "Optimizing the Educational Impact of a Museum Tour. *Curator* 27, no. 2 (1984): 135–40.

Schwartz, R. "Art Galleries and Museums: Nonclassroom Learning for the Nontraditional Student." *New Directions for Higher Education* 56 (1986): 69–75.

Seaman, Don, and Robert Fellenz. *Effective Strategies for Teaching Adults*. Columbus, Ohio: Merrill, 1989.

Simerly, R. G., and Associates, ed. *Handbook of Marketing Continuing Education*. San Francisco: Jossey-Bass, 1989.

Soren, B. "The Museum as Curricular Site." *Journal of Aesthetic Education* 26, no. 3 (1992): 91–101.

Spock, Michael. "On Beyond Now: Strategies for Assessing the Long Term Impact of Museum Experiences." Panel discussion notes, American Association of Museums Conference, Baltimore, Md., 2000.

Spock, Michael, and Debra Perry. "Listening to Ourselves: The Stories Museum People Tell and Their Implications for What Really Matters in Our Work." Paper presented at the annual meeting of the American Association of Museums, Atlanta, Ga., 1997.

Storr, A. V. F. "Current Practice and Potential: Research and Adult Education in Museums." U.S. Department of Education Conference Panel, 12–13 April 1995. Available: http://inet.ed.gov/pubs/PLLConf95/pelavin.html (1995).

Tarr, D. L. "Learning More about Your Market: Sources and Uses of Data." In *Handbook of Marketing for Continuing Education*, edited by R. G. Simerly, 30–48. San Francisco: Jossey-Bass, 1989.

Tough, Alan. *The Adult's Learning Projects*. Toronto: Ontario Institute for Studies in Education, 1971.

Valazquez, L. C. "New Market Audiences in Continuing Education." In *Organization and Administration of Continuing Education: A Textbook Designed to Facilitate Successful Programs and Processes in Adult and Continuing Education*, edited by V. W. Mott and L. C. Rampp, 145–62. Checotah, Okla.: AP Publications, 1995.

Williams, P. B. "Educational Excellence in Art Museums: An Agenda for Reform." *Journal of Aesthetic Education* 19, no. 2 (1985): 107–23.

Witkin, B. R. *Assessing Needs in Educational and Social Programs*. San Francisco: Jossey-Bass, 1984.

Wolins, I. S. "Teaching the Teachers." *Museum News* 69, no. 3 (1990): 71–75.

# INDEX

# ABOUT THE AUTHORS

**Dr. Bonnie Sachatello-Sawyer** is currently the director of Native Waters, an outreach program at Montana State University. She formerly served as the head of the education and public programs division at the Museum of the Rockies in Bozeman, Montana. She holds a doctorate in education from Montana State University.

**Dr. Robert A. Fellenz** is professor emeritus of adult education at Montana State University. From 1997 to 2000, he served as the lead adult education researcher at the Museum of the Rockies. He holds a doctorate in education from the University of Wyoming.

**Hanly Burton** is currently a third-year medical student at Western University College of Osteopathic Medicine in Pomona, California. From 1997 to 2000, he was an education research associate at the Museum of the Rockies. He holds a bachelor of science degree from the University of Wisconsin-Madison.

**Laura Gittings-Carlson** is the assistant curator of education at the Holter Museum of Art. She previously served as the assistant director of education at the Museum of the Rockies. She holds a bachelor of science degree from Montana State University.

**Janet Lewis-Mahony** works for the National Park Service in Yellowstone National Park. She completed a graduate internship at the Museum of the Rockies in 1997–99. She holds a master's degree in education from Montana State University.

**Walt Woolbaugh** is a junior high science teacher in the Manhattan School system, Manhattan, Montana. He also serves as an adjunct professor and teaching assistant in science methods, assessment, and action research classes at Montana State University. He is completing his doctorate at MSU.